2019
Writing from Inlandia

An Inlandia Institute Publication

Editorial Board

Publications Committee:
Chair: Mark Givens
Jack Belli, Judy Kronenfeld,
Christian Monroy, Victoria Waddle

2018-19 Inlandia Creative Writing Workshop Leaders:
Colton (bilingual): Jessica Carrillo
Corona: Andrea Fingerson
Ontario: Tim Hatch
Rancho Mirage & Palm Springs: Marj Charlier
Redlands: Mae Wagner
Riverside (RPL): Jo Scott-Coe
Riverside (Janet Goeske Center): CelenaDiana Bumpus
San Bernardino: Allyson Jeffredo & Romaine Washington

Poet-TRY online workshops
Stephanie Barbé Hammer

Executive Director
Cati Porter

Original Cover Design
Julie Frenznick

Book Layout & Design
Mark Givens

Editor
Cati Porter

ISBN: 978-1-7344977-3-1
© 2020 The Inlandia Institute and individual authors.
All rights reserved. All rights revert to author upon publication.
No part of this book may be reproduced without permission of the authors.

2019 WRITING FROM INLANDIA
Work of the Inlandia Creative Writing Workshops

This publication is the end result of a year of Inlandia Creative Writing Workshops held in eleven different locations across eight different cities in two counties, from libraries to senior centers, a museum, even online.

These workshops are part of the Inlandia Institute's Literary Professional Development Program, which also includes Boot Camp for Writers intensive workshops, Cartless writing workshops for our neighbors experiencing homelessness, and Tesoros de Cuentos, a workshop in the heart of Riverside's historic Casa Blanca community.

The purpose of this core program is to foster creative writing and support emerging and established writers of Inland Southern California at all skill levels—from beginners to intermediate practitioners to professional writers.

Workshop participants are diverse in age, gender, culture, and writing experience. Everyone has a story has to tell. We're here to help you tell it well.

CONTENTS

Colton at the Colton Area Museum
with Jessica Carrillo

Frances J. Vásquez
  Song of Praise for Ysabel and Margarita 14
Wil Clarke
  Flood on the Khami River 22
  Genealogy 25
Sylvia Nelson Clarke
  Crows 28
  Sister Summer in Montana 29
  Hit Me! 31
  Ferry Meeting: Two Views 32

Corona at the Corona Public Library
with Andrea Fingerson

Renee Gurley
  Love Changed My Face 36

Joslyn Joy Writers at Joslyn Senior Center in Redlands
with Mae Wagner

Margit Andersson
  To Go Home 42
Jerry Ellingson
  A New Mantra 43
  Where Earth and Heaven Met 50

Hazel Fuller
   Gerrards Market and S&H Green Stamps 54
   Miss Curry's Typing Class 57

Richard Hess
   She Fooled Me Again 60
   First Date 62

Rosalie Hruṣka
   Someday 64

Gary Neuharth
   Abstract Grace 65
   Lord Of The Rails 66
   Road Trip 68
   Stealer of Dreams 70
   Vampire Queen 72

Kristine Ann Shell
   The Wind 74
   On My Way Home 75

Ontario at the Ontario Public Library
with Tim Hatch

Tim Hatch
   PCH Sunset (New Year's Day, 2016) 78
   Oedipal Revenge Fantasy 79

Randy Quiroz
   The Boy Who Could Fly 81

Poets in Motion at the Janet Goeske Senior Center in Riverside
with CelenaDiana Bumpus

   Poets In Motion Unity Poem 2019 92

Sam Barclay
   Adventure Gone Awry 96

Victoria K. Begley
   First Choice 99
   My House 101

Mary Rodriguez Briggs
  Taco 102
  The Cantankerous Old Man's Paramour 105
  Voices 107

Georgette Buckley
  After The Rain 108
  S. Ana 109
  d'l'r'us 110
  @ d'l'r'us 111
  Flip-Flop 112

Natalie Michele Champion
  Alone 114
  Ethereal Life 115
  Follow the Raven 116
  Lost 117
  Our Bridge 118

Rick Champion
  Train To Salvation 119
  Strike 122
  If I was 124

Deborah Clifton
  Pure Adventure 125
  Pure Intention 126
  Merry Endeavors 127
  Vibrant 128
  Beloved Beauty 129

Aaron Craig
  The Sky Is Torn 130

Diana Dolphin
  Imagine This 131

Chuck Farrar
  Seascape 133

Constance Jameson
  The Long Road Part 1 136
  The Long Road Part 2 138
  Mirror, Mirror 139
  Pen 140
  Dream's Lament 141

Joan Jones
    Surplus—The Greatest Un-wash 142
    Unknown 144
    You Don't Matter 145
    Stop Hitching Your Wagon 147
    Still Here 148

Florence Lucero
    In Memory Of My Late Brother Eric 149
    Turning Point 150

Phyllis Maynard
    Fun Friday 151
    Tempest 154
    Celena's Mom 155

Vicki Urrunaga
    The Watcher 156
    Wobzec's State 157

Marlene Mossestad
    The Dream 158
    Scifaiku 159

Geri Olayan
    Last 160

Phyllis Ahpuck Reis
    The Spirit Of The Law 161
    The Letter Of The Law 163

Candace Shields
    Georgia's Little Red Riding Hood 165
    Mountains 174

Heather Takenaga
    Words 175

Gudelia Vaden
    Violet – The Fairy Princess 182
    The Wedding 184

Thomas Vaden
    An Ode to Whitney Houston 187
    Grandpa Bert's Dilemma 188
    Negotiation 190
    Truth Simplified 191

Alan Van Tassel and Sarah Van Tassel
   A Person In My Life 192
Jose Luis Vizcarra
   To Celena 200
   Regardless 201
Bobbie Walters
   A Lonely Visit Saved By Grandmother's Love 203
   A Lonely Visit At Aunt Aline's House 205
Jack Wilde
   The Turnout 207
   The Pacific Slide I 208

Poet-try Online
Stephanie Barbé Hammer

Cindi Neisinger
   Keto-Tass-Tic 210
S. J. Perry
   I'm Thinking of a Christmas 215

Riverside at the Riverside Public Library
with Jo Scott-Coe

CelenaDiana Bumpus
   First Clarinet 218
   Bird II 219
   These challenging days... (No rest for the ___) 220
   Meandering 221
Deenaz Coachbuilder
   Chambers of the heart 223
   Those Numbers 225
   Grace 227
   Fire and Earth 228
Carlos E. Cortés
   Ode to Baron Scarpia 230
   Gratitude: The Life of Carlos (With Apologies to Eric Idle) 232
   Out Of Order 233

Laurel Vermilyea Cortés
The Secret Life of Office Workers 235
On Being Laurel…And Yanny 236

Nan Friedley
Notes Are Still There 241
Losers 243
Triple Double Feature 245
@ Her 248

Christina Guillén
La Hada Orange Blossom 250
Everybody Okay 255

Robin Longfield
1964 (After Weldon Kees) 257
Bags 260
Before Blue 261

San Bernardino at the Rowe Branch of San Bernardino Public Library
with Allyson Jeffredo and Romaine Washington

Alben Chamberlain
On The Borderline 266
California Blowing 269
Christmas In The POW Camp 271

Charlotte LeVecque
Buffalo Stars 273
Ten 277

Jessica Lea Morgan
Resurrection Garden 280
Scents 281
electronic dusting 282
Haiku in Wrightwood 284
Quiet 285

S. J. Perry
Taking Down the Lights 287

Cindi Pringle
I Don't Wanna 288
Things to do in Hell 291

Carolyn Snow
Autumn Nights 293
Hair with Flair 294
The Invited Guest 295

Beth Winokur
A Response to Dr. Angelou's Pulse 299
Across the Water –No Boat Required 301

Author Biographies 305
About Inlandia Institute 315
Other Inlandia Books 316

COLTON AT THE COLTON AREA MUSEUM

with Jessica Carrillo

Frances J. Vásquez

Song of Praise for Ysabel and Margarita

The poetry of Las Cafeteras resounded, "Bailen, bailen mujeres de Luna / Bailen, bailen dejanse de contar," Spanish for "Dance, dance women of the moon / Dance, dance let yourself be counted."

While listening to the evocative melody and lyrics of "Mujeres de Luna", my imagination wondered. Visions emerged of two badass Mexican women from Casa Blanca who had the audacity to petition the Riverside City Board of Education — 109 years ago — because their children counted. They walked over four miles in the searing summer heat to request a neighborhood school for their children. The activist mothers served as Casa Blanca's culture bearers in pursuit of educational equity.

The July 11, 1911 minutes of the school board meeting state, "A petition was presented signed by eighty residents of Casa Blanca, asking for the erection of a public school in that locality. It appears that more than seventy children of school age reside in Casa Blanca: that forty children in primary grades now go to Victoria School."

The petitioners' names weren't deemed important enough to record in the school board minutes. Why? They also weren't identified in the Riverside Press Newspaper the following day, which reported, "A committee of two women from Casa Blanca appeared before the meeting of the board with a petition asking that some facilities be provided by the board for a school at Casa Blanca...." Could it have been the anti-Mexican sentiment of the era? Whatever the rationale, these two unnamed women were heroic — unsung SHEroes. They, along with the 80 signatories on the petition, served as Casa Blanca's culture bearers seeking equitable educational opportunities for their children. But social justice was elusive.

Two years later in 2013, at the behest of Stella Atwood, the sole female school board member, the District established makeshift classrooms for Casa Blanca kindergarten and first grade students in an old abandoned Prenda warehouse. Then, in 1918, the District moved the aged wooden structure to Madison Street in the center of Casa Blanca. Later, it burned down in early 1923 (soon after the Trustees had voted to hire a young Mabra B. Madden as Principal of the Casa Blanca School).

Finally, twelve years after the pivotal petition by *las Adelitas*, the school district at long last built a new Casa Blanca School in 1923. The plain, sturdy structure was designed by noted architect G. Stanley Wilson. It was built of reinforced concrete, a construction innovation at the time, and still stands today. In 1967, against the wishes of the Casa Blanca community, the District closed the public school to implement a storied **desegregation** program (utilizing one-way school busing of Casa Blanca students to no less than eight different schools). The busing of Casa Blanca students to various other schools continues to date. But not for long….

Justice is imminent: the Riverside Unified School District Board of Trustees voted unanimously to approve the purchase of property on Lincoln Avenue near Ysmael Villegas Park and SSgt. Salvador J. Lara Casa Blanca Library. "Somewhat uniquely, with Casa Blanca, the community has really treasured (a potential school) as part of their identity and their history," Board President Angelov Farooq stated on February 20, 2019 in The Press-Enterprise. "But the driving force is really the value it provides for students. We know neighborhood schools are good for student achievement, for the level of engagement it offers parents when it's conveniently accessible." Cindy Mendoza-Collins, current Chairwoman of the Casa Blanca Community Action Group (CAG) is diligently spearheading the community initiative.

In our quest to discover the women's identities, I enlisted help from the public and described the two mothers as "Adelitas de

Casa Blanca" in my Inlandia Literary Journeys Mothers Day column published on May 12, 2017 in The Press-Enterprise Newspaper. "We wish to offer flowers and tributes in their memory... precious turquoise gems." The mothers made an indelible mark in the history of education equity in Riverside. They are *tesoros* — cultural treasures on whose strong bronze shoulders have supported past and present community leaders that emerged in Casa Blanca and beyond.

Like history detectives, we resolved to discover their true identities — names which had become lost over time. After arduous research initiated by Roberto Murillo, we eventually pieced together the identity puzzle. **Ysabel Solorio Olvera and Margarita Salcedo Solorio** were identified as las *Adelitas* de Casa Blanca. Ecstatic, the community celebrates the two formidable *SHEroes* who led the 1911 grassroots campaign for a neighborhood school.

Why *Adelitas*? During the brutal Mexican Revolution (1910 to 1920) for agrarian reform and social justice, women *soldaderas* fought bravely alongside men. One famous *soldadera*, called *Adelita*, inspired a popular ballad named after her — thus, revolutionary women were often referred to as *Adelitas*. These female warriors inspired colorful folklore, stories, ballads, books, and movies.

The Revolution caused a large first wave of mass migration from México to the U.S. — including *las Adelitas* of Casa Blanca. The Olvera and Solorio families emigrated to Riverside at the beginning of the Revolution to seek employment and escape the ravages of war. There was little or no work to be had in war-torn México. In Riverside, there was an accelerated period of construction to support the lucrative citrus industry, which enabled Riverside to be named the wealthiest city per capita in the U.S.

Bill Wilkman, in "Casa Blanca's Evans Street" article in the February 2011 issue of JOURNAL of the Riverside Historical Society, cites oral history interviews conducted for the 2001 Casa Blanca historic properties survey: "Longtime elderly Casa

Blanca residents talked of whole families employed in agricultural pursuits, primarily related to the citrus industry. Family members worked in Evans Street corridor packing houses and picked fruit in area groves... the Evans Street corridor became the main locale for grocery stores, cafes, and purveyors of general merchandise.... It was in this economic environment that Casa Blanca grew and was solidified as a community... bound together primarily by three factors: proximity to the citrus industry, isolation from downtown Riverside, and the discriminatory practices of the day. Participants ... described a close knit community primarily consisting of persons of Hispanic, Italian, and Japanese origin."

Bill Wilkman suggests, "While the convenience of proximity to local stores and services undoubtedly kept many Casa Blanca residents close to home, discrimination also played a part for some of its residents. Oral history participants noted that barber shops outside of Casa Blanca would often refuse to serve non-Anglos. To meet the need for haircuts, Casa Blanca residents with barbering skills opened their homes on weekends as impromptu barber shops. The city's public swimming pools would not admit non-Anglos, so many Casa Blanca children used the irrigation canals as their 'swimming pools.'"

How did we identify las Adelitas?

Tesoros de Casa Blanca presented an exhibition of vintage school photos curated by Roberto Murillo at the beloved old Casa Blanca School building on May 21, 2017. The celebrated exhibition proved auspicious at many levels. Dr. Angelov Farooq, a Trustee with the Riverside Unified School District Board of Education and invited speaker, committed to work toward building a neighborhood school for Casa Blanca students. Anthony Rivera, then President of the Casa Blanca Community Action Group promised to make the Casa Blanca school a priority goal for the CAG.

Kimberly Olvera-Du Bry picked up a flyer about the exhibition and decided to go. She was the missing link! She later approached me to offer help with our Tesoros de Casa Blanca project.

Memories began to surface. Kimberly remembered the stories her great-grandmother Ysabel Solorio Olvera used to recount. Like regal Monarch butterflies, the Olvera family migrated approximately 1,700 miles from their hometown in Michoacán in South-West México to settle in Riverside.

Kimberly's great-grandfather Gaspar Olvera initially came to Riverside without his wife Ysabel. He had followed other family members who found work in the area. He lived in a labor camp in Casa Blanca until he saved enough money to bring Ysabel here. The couple eventually purchased a home on Railroad Street and raised a family in Casa Blanca.

Gradually, Kimberly remembered her Ita's (diminutive for abuelita) accounts of the arduous journey she and her *comadre* Margarita made to present the school petition. "Ita was always angry when she described how they walked all afternoon from Casa Blanca to downtown Riverside to attend the board meeting that evening." Kimberly recalls Ysabel as a "pragmatic, no-nonsense woman. She had a lot of dignity and felt outraged about the way they were treated. Ysabel was indignant that Casa Blanca students had to walk over a mile to school while the other kids had their own neighborhood schools. She declared, *'Didn't we all work and pay taxes like the others?'* To Ysabel this was an injustice."

After toiling all day in the packinghouse, Ysabel and her *comadre* Margarita — in the evenings and on Sundays — walked the neighborhood about the need for a local school, and gathered signatures for the petition. Apparently, a trusted advisor suggested the best way to convince school officials was to obtain signatures from all of the households in Casa Blanca. Most residents signed promptly — except for two. Ysabel went to the reluctant families several times to explain the importance of unity. We can surmise the fear residents may have felt about asserting themselves — some of the Trustees were their bosses. On the night before the school board meeting, Ysabel finally obtained the last two signatures.

Gaspar feared for his pregnant wife's safety and wellbeing,

given she was heavy with child. He tried to discourage her from attending the board meeting. However, Ysabel was determined. So, Gaspar, and his *compadre* Arnulfo Solorio, and a small group accompanied the brave mothers. The trolley that ran from Riverside to Corona and back on Magnolia Avenue bypassed them — didn't stop (after all, they were Mexicans...) Undeterred, the group trekked on foot in the sweltering heat to the Evans building in downtown Riverside, where the school board met at 7 p.m. in the office of W.A. Irving.

The discrimination they endured did not stop them. Gaspar spoke about angry white men harassing them while they waited outside, yelling, "Get out of here; you have no business here!" Gaspar stridently replied, "We do have business here — we're staying!"

Ysabel declared many times afterwards, "How dare the trolley not stop! They should treat everyone with respect." Kimberly asserts that her Ita never lost that fire, not even in her elderly years!

Kimberly reiterates, "Ysabel was a woman ahead of her time. She demanded to be treated with respect. As a Mexican immigrant woman of that era, she faced lots of barriers. At some point, it was too much to keep shouldering it, so she and her *comadre* took a stand. We could use more stories like this in the times we now live in, especially when we see and hear so much animosity and hate directed against immigrants. It makes me proud that Ysabel stood up for what was right — against a system that was oppressing her, her family, and her community. I think she's an inspiration, someone I can look back on and with whom I feel a connection. It's a story that I want to share and keep her memory and what she achieved alive."

In liz gonzález' book, "Dancing in the Santa Ana Winds: Poems y Cuentos New and Selected," her cuento poem "¡Vivan Las Mujeres!" resonates perfectly about the Olvera/Solorio saga: "Together our passion for social justice and equity, wisdom, and love are amplified. / The music of elder women's voices planning, catching up, and whispering secrets plays in the background …

/ lessons we learned from family women's sacred gatherings at the kitchen tables of our childhoods."

Trailblazers like Ysabel S. Olvera and Margarita S. Solorio are an inspiration to the community. They personify the best in human endeavor. Their legacy of fighting for education equity is valued. On December 11, 2019, the Casa Blanca Community Action Group paid homage to *las Adelitas de Casa Blanca* and their descendants. The festive event was supported by the Mayor of Riverside, International Relations Council, City Parks, Recreation and Community Services Department, Ramona High School Theater Arts Department, and *Comité las Adelitas de Casa Blanca*: Kimberly Olvera-DuBry, Roberto Murillo, Pete Trujillo, Frances J. Vásquez, and Liz Pinney-Muglia.

The community turned out with a pot-luck of favorite dishes in hand. Ramona High School Theater Arts students passionately re-enacted the 1911 Olvera/Solorio journey to the school board meeting. Their powerful performance brought chills and tears to many of us. The awesome *Mariachi Dinastía de Ramona High School* performed an array of delightful Mexican tunes to an appreciative audience. Importantly, extended family members connected and shared previously unseen photos and stories of their now renowned ancestors.

The motivating story of *las Adelitas* inspired the Multicultural Council of the Riverside Museum Associates to select the theme, "SHEroes and Heroes: Local Inspirations" for the 9th annual Day of Inclusion program in Riverside to honor the legacy of resilient, *unsung* community activists who made significant contributions to social justice and civil rights. The awe-inspiring event was celebrated at the historic Home Front at Camp Anza on December 14, 2019. Among several other amazing honorees, Ysabel and Margarita were feted for their trailblazing endeavors in education equity. A charming musical skit, performed by *Arlanza Teatro del Pueblo*, re-enacted the inspirational stories of local she/heroes of the past.

Riverside county's first Medal of Honor recipient, SSgt. Ysmael R. Villegas of Casa Blanca, last walked on *tierra firme* at

Camp Anza before he boarded ship en route to the Philippines where he died a gallant hero during World War II. It seemed as if Ysmael's luminous spirit was there in the beautifully renovated officers club smiling with gratitude along with all of our departed and present-day SHEroes and HEroes.

¡Bravas, Ysabel S. Olvera and Margarita S. Solorio — you count and your story matters!

WIL CLARKE

Flood on the Khami River

> ²When thou passest through the waters, I will be with thee; and through the rivers, they shall not overflow thee: when thou walkest through the fire, thou shalt not be burned; neither shall the flame kindle upon thee.
> Isaiah 43:2 King James Version (KJV)

In late December 1971, at the height of the rainy season, Sylvia, two-year-old Esther, and I spent Christmas with my parents who were working at Solusi College. My father, C. Fred, and mother, Esther, had gone to Africa as missionaries in 1936. Amongst many other things they had done in Africa, they had created this four-year university college in the bush about 30 miles west of Bulawayo, Zimbabwe's second largest city. Fred, now 66 years old, had returned to Solusi to build up a science program, and Esther, only 2 years his junior, was teaching what would have been a double load of English classes in an American university. These white-haired, seasoned missionaries were taking us in to the Bulawayo Airport on the second leg of our trip back to the States on furlough from our five year stint as freshman missionaries to Tanzania.

In those days the Khami Road leaving Bulawayo was paved for about two miles and then continued as two tarred strips for another three miles before Solusi's dirt road turned off and continued west to the College. The general slope of the countryside was north towards the Zambezi River some 270 miles away. That meant all of the local rivers flowed northwards, and the Solusi road crossed several of them. Each river crossing was made on a concrete "drift" built on the river bed that facilitated an easy crossing during dry season. Mother joked: "If you fall into an African river, simply get up, brush the dust off, and go on your way."

The rivers, however, could be treacherous during the rainy season. The F. H. Muderspachs, veteran missionaries from Norway to Uganda, had recently tried to cross an African river and had died when their car was washed downstream. So we always approached flooded rivers with great caution. These rivers had a nasty habit of washing out one end or the other of the drift and carving out a deep channel that couldn't be seen while the river was in flood.

On our way to the Bulawayo Airport, we successfully forded the largest of these rivers, the Gwaai River. On the other hand, the Khami River, the last river before getting onto Khami Road, was flooded. No one had any idea whether it had washed a nasty channel across its drift or not, so we pulled over to one side and discussed our predicament. The only other possibility would be to go back to Solusi and then go south to the little railroad siding town of Figtree and take the Plumtree Road into Bulawayo. But that was many miles out of our way and would be slow; we probably would not get to the airport in time for our flight.

Then a rickety old bus pulled up beside us. The driver waved, and we waved back. He gingerly drove into the river and slowly crept across. Obviously the Khami River was deep, but the crossing was still intact. Finally the bus pulled over to the left hand side and waited for us.

Dad, with a confidence he didn't feel, said, "Let's try it!" Claiming the promise in Isaiah 43:2, "When thou passest through the waters, I will be with thee; and through the rivers, they shall not overflow thee," he cautiously entered the river. The Peugeot station wagon got in deeper and deeper until the muddy waters came over the headlights. It was very fortunate that his wagon had a diesel engine; if it had been gasoline, the wet spark plugs would have shorted out, and we might well have suffered the Muderspachs' fate. Several times we caught our breath as the wagon started to drift sideways downstream, but the wheels caught again, and we proceeded on across. Dozens of curious bus riders stared out their windows at us.

As we pulled up on the Bulawayo side of the river, the bus passengers all cheered! I only wish I had known enough Ndebele to understand what they were saying. Water poured out from every nook and cranny of the station wagon. Heading toward town, we thanked God. And yes, we arrived at the airport in time for our flight.

WIL CLARKE

Genealogy

My thirteen year-old niece, Andi Clarke, came to visit us in Massachusetts during the summer in 1984. Like most of the Clarkes, she has a huge intellectual curiosity about everything you could imagine. One day she asked me, "Do you know anything about our ancestors?" I told her I had a few names of our ancestors on my Dad's side of the family and an obituary of a great-great-grandfather on my mother's side.

I had quizzed my paternal aunt, and she told me what she knew about the family ancestors, which eventually was very helpful, but also wrong. I had also inherited from my Mother a copy of a *Biographical Sketch of George Washington Willard* written in 1899 by my great-aunt Mary's daughter, Mrs. J. W. Teasdale. It turned out that George was my great-great-grandfather. He had owned part or all of some 48 steamboats on the Mississippi River, "some of them the largest and finest that came to the St. Louis levee. During the civil war he was a determined and consistent Union man, with strong personal sympathies for his friends in the south. In his boating expeditions he was sometimes forced to serve one side as well as the other. These experiences were not agreeable to Captain Willard who had been accustomed to command, rather than to be commanded, and in 1863 he disposed of his steamboat interests"[1] and bought a large farm near Centralia, Illinois. He was a founder and staunch member of the third Baptist church in Centralia and its wealthiest member.

A few days after Andi's question, I went down to the Lancaster, Massachusetts, public library and asked the librarian what I could do to find my ancestors. She sneered in gross disgust and

---

[1] *Biographical Sketch of George Washington Willard* by Mrs J. W. Teasdale in 1899

in a strong English accent told me to consult the card catalog. I quickly learned that a lot of professional librarians despise and hate genealogists.

Ignoring her insulting attitude, I went to the card catalog looking for the names I had. Starting down the list alphabetically with Barnhurst, Clarke, etc., I found nothing on any of them. Finally I reached Willard and struck pay dirt. The library had a book entitled *Willard Genealogy* by Charles Henry Pope, published in Boston in 1915. It was in the library because Willard was one of the founders of Lancaster, Massachusetts, way back in 1653. Looking through the index, I found a George Washington Willard. It gave his birth date and then made a statement to the effect that G. W. Willard, while still a young man, had moved west, and all contact with him had been lost. He had the same birth date as the one listed in my obituary as well as a few other facts about his life that were the same. I assumed I had found my ancestor.

Approaching the same librarian with an English accent about a founder of Lancaster, I found that, between steaming cups of fragrant tea, she became cheerful and very helpful. She showed me a set of four three-ring binders assembled in 1942: *Early Families of Lancaster, 1643 – 1700* by Frederick Lewis Weiss, minister of the First Church of Christ in Lancaster. It traced the ancestry of 50 of the early founders of the town. This was a veritable wealth of my ancestors. All of a sudden I realized that I had come home. Lancaster was where many of my ancestors from England had settled. There they farmed. There some of them built garrison homes. Many of them fought the Indian raiders. Some of them were killed and scalped by those raiders.

One of them was a sawyer, Tom Sawyer, who not only built a sawmill in Lancaster but also his own garrison home there. At one point he was captured and tortured by warriors of King Philip—an Indian chief who fought a protracted war against the settlers. While Tom was still a captive, the Indians took him up to Quebec and eventually tied him to a stake and piled fagots up around him intending to burn him alive. They could almost smell the smoke of his torment when the local French priest marched up to the site with a huge procession of believers and confronted the Indians with threats of eternally burning hellfire. So they made a deal for his life. Part of the deal was that Tom Sawyer would build a sawmill for the city. This was the first sawmill in Quebec and possibly in Canada. The complete adventures of Tom and his son Tom Sawyer Jr. would fill a book and make an interesting read.

The notebooks of the town's founders enabled me to trace my ancestry back to William the Conqueror, Charlemagne, Old King Cole, Robert the Bruce King of Scotland, and even the despicable Roman Emperor Tiberius who crucified Jesus Christ. I once shared my findings with my cousin Bobbie Marie who lamented: "Can't you find any of our ancestors who were respectable?" I loved it.

I am descended from a whole bunch of rogues as well as great men and women. One of my distant cousins was Francis E. Willard, founder of the American Women's Christian Temperance Union (WCTU). Another prominent ancestor/cousin was the great champion of the environment, especially Yosemite National Park, John Muir.

For months I made time to return to the library at least weekly in pursuit of more family history. Eventually I shared my findings with my niece, Dr. Andrea Clarke M.D., who probably feels that I provided far more than she ever wanted to know.

Sylvia Nelson Clarke

Crows

A crew of crows cruises neighborhoods;
    Raucous cawing announces the crowd.
One with a morsel others deem good
    besieged by its fellows, crying loud.

Do crows just scout in selected cliques?
    Share territory? Understand words?
Teach each other a grand mix of tricks?
    What crimes do they create, crafty birds?

A hawk, chased by rasping ravens, dives
    among leafy branches, hunkers down.
A cacophonic black cloud arrives,
    swirls in protest till all trees they crown.

Yet no crowing makes enemy budge,
    so one by one, they rise and take flight,
Sinking sun giving each a small nudge
    to wing to the riverbed for night.

Cawing,
    Raucous,
        Omnivorous, they
            Wing their way
                Steadily home.

Sylvia Nelson Clarke

Sister Summer in Montana

The summer of 1952 Daddy had just finished his first year of teaching. I was almost ten, my sister Elvina five and a half, and Mama was feeling a bit queasy. I didn't know it then, but teaching contracts only paid for nine months, so my parents must have wondered how to survive the summer without pay. We ended up in Butte, Montana, where their friends, George and Genevieve Beech, ran the Summit Valley Sanitarium.

Did we get free board and room? Perhaps. Ginny, before she married George, had been the nurse who treated patients that came to Melrose Sanitarium where Dad and Mom worked before Daddy went to college. She and her daughter, Betty Jean, lived with Mama and me some of the time when Daddy was away in the Army. Later they visited Mama when she had my little sister, Elvina, in the Butte hospital.

This Montana summer, Elvina was going on six, quite independent, and almost fearless. Two incidents show this. One day Elvina helped herself to some coins from the Pomade can that held church offering money. Then without asking permission, she and Daryl, a boy about her age who was visiting the San, walked to a nearby store and bought gumdrops and pink bubble gum. I don't remember what kind of discipline our parents chose for her.

Another time, when Betty Jean, now college age, took us for a day at the amusement park, we rode on the carousel and later took a stomach-lurching ride on the roller coaster. I was dismayed when Elvina begged, "Let's do it again!" She hadn't been afraid at all!

Betty smiled, but I hung back. "I'd rather ride the carousel again," I told Betty. So she and Elvina patiently guided me to the carousel. Once they saw me safely seated on a painted zebra, they ran back to catch the next coaster ride. Maybe they enjoyed it, but once was enough for me!

One afternoon, Daddy was working out in front of the Sanitarium planting pansies along the walkway. Elvina and I were there trying to help. "What do we put in next? Yellow or purple ones?" I moved to the flat of pansies sitting on the path.

"Yellow, please," Daddy smiled at me. "We just put in a purple one."

I handed him a yellow pansy plant then turned to see what my sister was watching. There by the far corner of the building stood the regular gardener smoking a cigarette. "Chimney nose. Chimney nose! You have a chimney nose," Elvina chanted, pointing at him.

"Shhh! Don't say that! That's not nice," I chided, my face turning red. I recognized the phrase from a verse I learned at school:

Tobacco is a filthy weed
and from the devil doth proceed.
It picks your pockets, burns your clothes,
and makes a chimney of your nose.

I had taught it to her so felt partly responsible for her thoughtless taunt.

Another time Elvina went missing. Mama and Daddy and I started looking everywhere inside and outside the building. Finally I saw her slouched under a small table in the basement, a bottle of rubber cement glue spilling out on the floor from her slack hand. "I found her," I cried.

Daddy came quickly and picked Elvina up. I followed him and Mama as they carried her up the stairs, out the door, and into the fresh air. They laid her on the grass where both Mama and Daddy knelt over her, trying to get her to respond. Eventually she opened her eyes and tried to sit up.

We all breathed a sigh of relief.

I learned a lesson from my little sister that day: Sniffing glue is a bad idea.

Sylvia Nelson Clarke

Hit Me!

Sixth grader Vicki stalked around the playground, a scowl on her face as she repeatedly smacked her right fist into her left palm. Coming closer, Teacher Merrill heard her mutter, "I'd sure like to hit somebody." Smack! Smack! "Wish I could hit someone."

Instead of asking who or why, Teacher commented, "So you want to hit someone?" and added,

"Here, you can hit me," and indicated the middle of his back.

Vicki looked surprised. "Yeah, but . . . ."

"Go ahead. Hit me!" Teacher encouraged. So with her fist, Vicki hauled off and punched him hard in the back.

"Ow! Ooow!" Vicki backed away rubbing her hand. Why had it hurt so much?

"Oh, I'm sorry," Teacher apologized. "That was my steel back brace you hit. I didn't expect you to hit so hard."

Vicki shook her head in disbelief as she nursed the sore fist. Never again did she talk about wanting to hit someone at school. Who knew what secret might make it dangerous?

Sylvia Nelson Clarke

Ferry Meeting: Two Views

I'm here by Staten Island Ferry waiting for Judith, my mother. She arranged with Dad to meet me here after the Thanksgiving parade. It was okay as Macy's parades go, but I've seen so many—almost every year since I was little enough to sit on Dad's shoulders.

Last night Dad said, "Remember, Son, your mother's meeting you at the ferry tomorrow. Dress up in your school uniform—jacket and all. It'll be cold out there." As if I didn't know. I'm 12 already! I can take care of myself. Besides, I want Mother to be proud of me, too.

We're almost like strangers. She left when I was about three. Every other month or so we meet somewhere uptown, at a museum, or in a park—never at her apartment or my house. I'd like to show her my room, model planes I made, and my book collection. She'd be sure to like that. She tells me interesting details about history, the city, so she must read a lot.

There she is. That's her in the big fur coat. Maybe Jim got it for her birthday—in July? Ah! She sees me now. Do I hug her or shake hands?

How will I find him in all these crowds? It's not that I won't recognize him—but he is shooting up so tall these days. Let's see, was it August when we last met? Oh dear! And he's twelve now. He might be almost as tall as I am.

Why should I worry? He's always been at our meeting place on time before. I recognize him by his stance—so straight and tall.... Is it as much a duty for him as I sometimes feel? (Sigh) He can't understand why I left him and his father—was it nine years ago?—probably never will.

At least I keep in touch—Oh! There he waits like a sentry at his post. He's seen me. Can I still hug him, or would he prefer a handshake?

"Hello, Son. Ready for a cruise around the harbor with me as your tour guide?"

CORONA AT THE CORONA PUBLIC LIBRARY

with Andrea Fingerson

Renee Gurley

Love Changed My Face

I have never liked getting my picture taken. While other girls were spraying, combing and coifing in the bathroom for picture day in high school, I was hiding out at the school smoking corner hoping no one noticed that I skipped my picture time. No one ever did notice. My picture did not appear in my high school yearbook until senior year when my mom forced me into a senior picture photoshoot. I shudder even now at the thought of these pictures where I tried to use eye liner to hide my face from the camera lens. I don't like those pictures to this day.

My hairdresser, Jon, did never knew how camera shy for the first decade he cut my hair. He learned on the first date we went on. I knew he relied on a camera to compensate for the 5 brain surgeries he'd undergone for a brain tumor he'd had since his early twenties. He was a bit surprised when he pulled his camera out as we walk around Lake Arrowhead. I covered my face and said, " No, no, no!" He put down his camera and apologized. He wasn't used to this. His ex-wife had been a woman whose vanity some say led her to leave him. .

He would ask questions about this on dates that followed. .

"Why don't you like pictures of yourself?"

"I don't know" was my standard answer.

However, I did know.

I didn't like my face.

I mean, it was an okay face…nothing really glaringly wrong with it…mouth a little thin, nose a little pointy, eyes pretty okay, pain in the ass eyebrows topped by entirely too much hair. I was no uglier than any other women, nor pretty, but there was just something about my face I didn't like. I couldn't pinpoint it, but I did know that pictures were simply a reminder that there was something wrong, so I avoided them every single time someone pulled a camera out.

Now, one would think Jon, who had fallen in love with me, would have been sympathetic towards my dislike for the lens; however, he was the exact opposite. Within the first couple months of dating him, he discovered the two pictures of myself I hated the most.

The first was my driver's license photo. To understand me on any level, you must know one thing…I DEPLORE the DMV…sure, yeah, some people claim to not like it, but I DEPLORE it…I come undone. The day I had my DMV photo taken was no different. I had gone early in the morning to try to beat the ghetto crowd of Riverside CA but found myself behind some belligerent woman who was threatening to kick the DMV's clerks' ass and she was taking entirely too long doing so. Thus, needless to say, when I had my ID picture taken, I was pissed, and it shows. When Jon found this picture of me, he laughed his ass off and when he found out I had a duplicate ID with the same picture, he took a push pin and hung my duplicate on the wall that faced my front door when I opened it. Every time I returned to my house, I would open my door and was forced to look what Jon liked to call, "my angry little face."

Then, there was the passport picture. This picture is one of the worst photos I have ever taken. It was taken when I was 33 and had moved back to Colorado for a year to help my mom with a divorce. It was the worst year of my life. I got to see to the extent to which I was neglected as a kid. A man who was a friend and someone I loved on a core level killed himself and my entire family was going bat shit crazy. I felt more alone, angry and hopeless than I had ever felt in my life. A perfect time for a picture. So, there I am. Hair in braids, pasty white (Colorado is void of light) and the look of a woman heading into a life of bitterness and Bacardi 151 shots for breakfast. When Jon first saw this picture, he actually was quiet for a moment but then, he laughed and said, "Wow, that is one of the worst pictures I have ever seen of anybody.…I call this one Angry Heidi." Thanks, Jon. After this, you would think Jon would have had sympathy for this photo. No. Instead he used this photo as arsenal. Believe it or not, there were times when Jon and I argued. Often when this would happen, Jon would run to the closet shelf where I kept my passport, he would grab it and open it like it was a mouth. Then, he would chase me around the house with passport and say, "Ewwwww….look…it's Angry Heidi! What does Angry Heidi have to say? Ewwww…Angry Heidi is angry."

My reaction to this was unpredictable. Sometimes when he would do this, I would get even more pissed at him; other times it made me laugh and the fight would be over.

Jon and I's fights were few and far between. What went on between us most of the time was love. At the end of the day, we would often just lie around, kiss each other and tell each other about our day. We had this little ritual from the first day we started dating. Early on in the relationship, I remember filling these conversations with the negative parts of my day or life. I would tell him how somebody pissed me off or how my mother was. I also remember Jon reaching over and pulling me into a hug and whispering, "More light, Gurley, less dark." At first, I felt angry with him that he didn't want to hear my problems; however, as I went further into love with Jon, I realized it wasn't that he didn't want to hear the negative things. He had plenty of negative things in his life: a twenty some odd year battle with a terminal illness that took everything…Jon had some shit, but he rarely filled our daily love check ins with these topics. What he did do was fill these daily love check-ins with was love. He would talk about how much he loved certain people in his life; he would talk about a food he loved or a song. He focused on the love while I focused on the crime.

And I cannot tell you when it happened. Maybe it was when Jon hung his duplicate ID picture next to mine in our hallway and every time I walked into the house, I had to face "my angry little face" next to what Jon liked to call, "his happy little face." Maybe it was watching a man go through hell with his health and heart and who still always seemed to be beaming. It was, I don't know, but I do know this…something happened.

The first time I noticed it was in a certain picture of Jon and me. It was taken by Jon's neuro-surgeon, Dr. Hsu. Hsu, like everyone else that came into contact with Jon, fell in love with him. When he found out that Jon was putting together a website to document his cancer journey, Hsu ushered his medical assistants out of the room, leaned over towards us and said,

"I usually keep my personal life and professional life separate but personally, I am a photographer and I would love to take some pictures for your website."

Jon and I were honored by Hsu's offer and three weeks later, we took his daughter down to Hsu's beach condo/photo studio. It was there we spent the afternoon. Hsu took many pictures of Jon and his daughter who wore a beautiful dress. Both of them naturals to the camera…all smiles and beauty. I sat on the sidelines, observed and prayed that Hsu wouldn't invite me into the action. Yet, it was inevitable.

"Your turn, Renee," he said.

Jon piped in, "Come on, Renee."

I shuddered at the thought. I could see us getting these beautiful pictures of Jon and his daughter but then there would be pictures of me and that damn face of mine. I tried to get out of this photo opportunity; however, I knew it might be unwise to piss your boyfriend's neuro-surgeon off, so after a bit of a fight, I complied. When I did, Jon sat on this red couch with me. I closed my eyes and a picture as taken.

When Jon and I got the photos back, we went to Border's to look at the pictures Hsu sent. We sat over two coffees ewwing and ahhing at the amazing pictures Hsu had taken…they captured Jon. Then, come the picture of Jon and me. We both looked at it. I was waiting for the familiar feeling of self-hate, but as I looked at that photo, self-hate never stirred. Instead Jon put his hand on my knee and whispered,

"Gurley, look, your face has changed."

I couldn't help but agree. Gone was the tight little mouth, the nose wasn't so pronounced, the eyes had kindness. This was a woman in love and next to this woman in love was Jon's "happy little face." It is the first picture of myself that I didn't completely hate.

Jon has been dead for awhile now; Much has changed. However, you will still never see me standing in line at Glamour Shots. Yet, friends and family have captured my face a time or two since Jon's death. Every time they do, I still cringe; I still have that feeling of taking an eyeliner to my face. However, when I open up those photo attachments in my email or Facebook account, I can see that Jon's love is still with me. How? I see it in my face. It has changed. What was the change? Love. Love changed my face. If love can do that, I can't help but wonder what else love can do...

JOSLYN JOY WRITERS AT JOSLYN SENIOR CENTER IN REDLANDS

with Mae Wagner

Margit Andersson

To Go Home

Now there is only an illusion left, and a memory. To try to go home is to grasp at misty swirls covering a landscape that doesn't exist. It flows through the fingers, nothing is concrete, not people, not time, not a culture. Yet in your memory, it is all engraved, as if etched in stone.

Then you realize that even your memory is not a true reflection of the way it was, maybe the way you want it to be so you can have peace. Time has imperceptibly altered and changed some of your perspectives and compromised your memories. Nostalgia has crept in, distorting the picture you wanted to retain.

Truth is, home never was what you might now try to resurrect in your mind's eye. The reality then was not a play performed for future dreams and comforting illusions. It had unspeakable darkness, conflicts and despair. It had a light as a guide so you could see a little bit in front of you, as well.

This is all very abstract, but these allegories are what I must resort to when describing what is impossible, to try to go home after you have left.

JERRY ELLINGSON

A New Mantra

"Hey, Mike, are you going to do the Dolphin Run?"

"If coach says, 'run', I run," Mike hollered across the grade school gymnasium and then immediately turned his attention back to us. "We're going to the tables at the back of the room. This is the first place you will go when you get here Saturday mornings. Pick up one of everything." He stopped briefly, turned halfway so he could look at us directly and said, "These are from coach. He o.k.'s everything before it goes on this table. If it's here, it's part of the training. If he says, 'Do it.', do it. If you follow everything he tells you to do, you'll be ready for the marathon in March. Come on, I'll show you how the table is laid out and explain the materials to you."

He turned back again towards the rear of the gymnasium and started pushing his way through the crowd: a young man in his late 20's or early 30's with dark hair and olive skin – he was only about 5 foot nine, but his body was nothing but muscle. *He must do more than just run to have that great of a body*, I thought.

I threw a quick look at my daughter, Heather, to find her staring at me with her mouth slightly open as if she was about to say something, but all that came out of the round circle of her lips was a whispered, "Wow." Afraid of losing Mike, our newfound friend of four minutes, in the crowd, we both plunged forward through the metal folding chairs; the people in small and large groups, talking and laughing, while sometimes blocking the way and sometimes moving in a slow herd as others were flitting through everything and everyone - sometimes with papers in their hands, having reached the table and accomplished task number one on this first training day in preparation for the LA Marathon on March 2, 1997.

* * * *

One Saturday, about three weeks earlier, Heather and I were having lunch at South Coast Plaza during a shopping day at Nordstrom. She was quiet for a few moments with an obvious change of conversation on her mind.

"Mom, I know this might sound silly to you, but there are some things I want to do before I'm thirty."

"I don't think that's silly. You should have goals all through your life. They're changeable. You should also make sure you get some things done while you can. Don't let dreams and plans slip away from you."

Heather relaxed in her chair and smiled.

"What would you like to do before you're thirty," I asked

"I want to run a marathon." The words began to just tumble out of her mouth. Now it was my turn to be surprised. Heather had never been athletic. Her small motor skills had developed early in her life. When she was three, we had to search everywhere for scissors small enough to fit her tiny hands, while sharp enough to actually cut as finely as her creative mind required. Her large motor skills were secondary in her growth. When she was four, she had an imaginary jump rope in her dress pocket because she couldn't get the hang of using a real one; but her use of fine brushes and paints was incredible. When she was seven, despite all efforts of family, friends and neighbors, she was so shaky on a bicycle, her first grade teacher asked for a private conference so she could discreetly find why Heather had so many bruises on her body. Another reason a marathon was a surprising choice to me was because the day we were spending at South Coast Plaza was what Heather was all about – stylish clothes, cosmetics, great hair and shopping for great bargains – not dumpy workout clothes, tennis shoes and a sweaty body.

She began to tell me how she had heard about the LA Road Runners program on the techno radio station she listened to in the car. Participants met in Santa Monica every Saturday morning and trained with a coach and then trained on their own during the week. She had been listening to the ad over and over and had now decided she really wanted to do it.

Heather stopped talking, sat back in her chair, looked at me with raised eyebrows and said, "What do you think?"

I didn't want to pause for long, because I was afraid Heather would take my lack of immediate, enthusiastic answer as doubt or disapproval I might have of her choice. That was not at all what was happening. The whole time Heather was talking at Mach speed, my mind was whizzing through everything she was saying and beyond to something I had been agonizing over. Maybe this was the answer I needed to solve my problem.

I had been too afraid to tell anyone in my family, but at fifty-seven, I had been having some strange signs that I knew were issues. I would have to deal with them, but they were too upsetting to address. Sometimes I would be awakened from a deep sleep with a heartbeat that was so loud and strong, it was like something from the percussion section of an orchestra. Often my heartbeat would be strong enough to hear, and then it would just stop. That was scary and really got my attention. What was scarier was when it didn't start beating again. I began to count how long it was between beats. Sometimes it was five seconds 10 seconds, more, less. It was irregular. Once it was sixty-five seconds. A few weeks of this and I was more than a little nervous. I knew I had to do something. I knew I should see a doctor. Maybe this was a choice thrown right in front of me.

"Do you mind if I do it with you?"

* * * *

As Mike walked us to the front of the room to find a seat in one of the metal folding chairs at the front of the grammar school gymnasium, his final piece of advice was to be sure we came back to the grammar school at the end of training to pick up water and a banana.

The room was filled beyond capacity. Coach came to the front of the stage and began to go through the paperwork Mike had helped us pick up at the back of the room. I fell in love with Coach from the moment I first saw him.

He was tall and slender – all muscle – somewhere in his sixties with a very cheery face and upbeat attitude. As a young man, he had competed as a Marathon runner in the LA Olympics. Later, he became a Los Angeles police officer and was soon assigned to train the new recruits. He had just recently retired from the police force, but his connection to the Academy would benefit us later on during our training year.

After a brief overview of the routine for Saturday and an explanation of the schedule for the upcoming months we held in our hands, we all left the building to begin our new adventure.

We all walked or jogged the five minutes from the school to Venice Beach. Coach was waiting for us. He introduced the doctor and the physical therapist to us. Both of them would be available on Saturdays for any questions or advice. The physical therapist led us in some warm-up exercises and then the group faced North and approximately 1200 people began to move up the Venice Beach Strand. Coach faced us, high-fiving everyone as they passed by him. We didn't know it then, but no matter how long it took each of us to finish the Marathon, he would be there to welcome us across the finish line in the same way.

The veteran runners took off. A smaller group of new people, including Heather and me, began walking together, introducing ourselves to one another and chatting as we walked.

At 7 o'clock in the morning on the Strand there are very few tourists. Most of the Venice people were busy setting up their booth or space along the sidewalk. Some of them were still sleeping, with heads on rolled up coats or jackets for pillows. Some of them had a torn sleeping bag or an old blanket, while some had nothing to cover them at all. Between now and March there would be no more sleeping in on Saturday mornings for those living on Venice Beach.

After a while, something strange began to happen to me. On one of my shoulders was a little white angel. On the other shoulder was a little devil in red and black. They were both talking in my ears. I kept thinking they would go away because it was just something I was imagining. But they stayed and they continued to argue with me. The angel kept telling me to continue on because I was doing a good thing and I was going to be healthy; this was going to be great. The devil kept telling me that I could just go home if I wanted to. I didn't have to stay here. I didn't have to do this. Surely they weren't really here. That was impossible. But they just kept talking into my ears. After a few minutes, I grabbed Heather by the wrist and pulled her back just a little bit so that we were away from the crowd.

"Heather, do I look different? Do you notice anything strange about me?"

Heather looked me up and down with a questioning face, and then she said, "Do you mean other than the fact that you don't have any makeup on and your hair hasn't been curled?"

"No, I already know that. I mean anything unusual, anything you've never seen about me."

"No. Can you give me a clue, Mom?"

"Well, if you can't see it, I guess I'm okay. It's just that I have a little angel on one shoulder and a little devil on the other shoulder and I wasn't sure if other people could see them or not. I guess they can't."

"Well, said Heather, that's kind of cool. What do they look like?"

"They are about three inches tall. The angel is, of course, all dressed in white with blonde hair white wings. You know, just like one of those cherubic angels that sit on top of a Christmas tree. She is so positive, it's sickening."

Heather started laughing. "You mean she sounds like you when we tease you about being a Pollyanna?"

"Do I really sound that bad?" I asked.

"Yeah, said Heather. But don't worry about it Mom, you're always right, so we get over it."

"She is so sappy, I just want to do the opposite of what she wants me to do, even though I know she's right. On the other hand, the little devil is pretty annoying, too."

"What does he look like?" asked Heather.

"Oh, you know. He looks like any other devil. He's all in black with little horns on his head, a black cape with red lining and, of course, a pitchfork. He is a smooth talker. He keeps telling me that I don't have to do this. We have time to go home, take a shower, have a little nap, go to lunch and maybe do a little shopping. He's like a guy you would meet in a bar that thinks he's sweet talking his way into your pants, but is just so transparent he's ridiculous. I just want to keep on going to spite him."

"I can go either way, Mom. Just tell me what you want to do."

"I have to tell you, I really am hating this." I looked at my watch. "We only have about 10 more minutes before we turn around to start back. I don't want to miss my banana and water. Let's just go for it."

And so we finished our first Saturday of training. We made a lot of new friends that day. Runners are so social with a huge variety of personalities and lots of interests.

We started a new tradition that first Saturday. It would continue through our Saturdays as we trained. On our way home from LA, we drove through McDonald's and picked up an orange juice and an English muffin with butter and honey, to munch on our way home. After a shower and a short nap, we found we had a lot of new energy. The positive rewards of our training had started.

During training, Sunday would always be a light day; a recovery day. Coach had told us how to get started. He said to run as long as we could before we ran out of breath. Then we would check the time on our watch, and split the time in half. If our training for the day was for 30 minutes, we would run for half the time, and walked half the time. For example: if we could run for 10 minutes before we ran out of breath, we would walk for five minutes and then run for five minutes, alternating this pattern for the 30 minutes. With my watch in hand, I began to run until I couldn't run anymore. I stopped my watch looked at the time, and was dumbfounded. My time was 27 seconds. I just stood there and looked at my watch, not knowing what to do. Was I supposed to split 27 seconds? Well, I thought, "If coach says do it, I'll do it." So I set my watch for 13 second intervals, and that first day of training on my own: a thirty minute workout consisting of thirteen seconds running and thirteen seconds walking. Each week we would repeat the process, and each week our walk/run time would increase. Now, I was really on my way.

Jerry Ellingson

Where Earth and Heaven Met

He was 21 years old when he saw the movie, *Windjammer*, a Cinerama film billed as Cinemiracle. It was a documentary of a Tall Ship as it travelled on the high seas. He immediately fell in love with the ocean, this young man, raised on the prairies of Alberta, Canada: the ocean he had never seen except on a giant movie screen.

Now, on what would have been his sixty-sixth birthday, I brought his ashes from where we had lived for only five, short months in Canada, back to where we had spent over forty years of our married life in California – the place where his love of sailing on the ocean had given him such complete joy and satisfaction.

It was March. The sky was blue with white clouds and the ocean was calm, even past the breakwater. It was a perfect day. I felt strangely serene that day. It was just a month and two days since Harvey had died. I had been so lonely without him. Others were kind and loving and there for me. But inside, I was alone. The piece of him that had become a part of me was missing. Grief made me feel as if I had been wrapped very tightly in saran wrap. I could see others and they could see me, but the restrictiveness of the sensation of being bound created a suffocation that seemed to barely allow enough breath to continue to breathe. Life had become rote – one foot in front of the other – no allowance for any thoughts or emotions. It is impossible to continue this way for very long, and so sometimes, without any warning, I would burst from the tight restraint with sobs and floods of tears. Tightly wrapped saran wrap can't hold one together forever. But today, I didn't feel bound. I felt free of constraints around my body and around my heart. I felt serene. I felt that he was with me, and this is where he wanted to be.

As I neared the dock, Bob and his partner, Dave, were busy with final preparations on Bob's boat to take everyone out on the water. Larry came towards me from his slip. He and Warren wanted to use their boat for our special trip, but they were in the middle of some major renovations, and they couldn't be ready in time. Larry greeted me with so much tenderness. He is one of the kindest persons I have ever met. He asked me to come over to their boat for a moment. He had bought some white roses and spent the morning removing the petals so we could mix them with the ashes to mark the spot on the water, if that was o.k. with me. That's one of the beautiful things about Larry – he wanted to be certain that it was alright rather than just imposing his ideas on me. He was also so excited to show me the work they had done on the boat, because theirs was the boat Harvey loved the most. After we toured the boat and picked up the rose petals, Larry guided me to the end of the slip to show me something very special. The symbol flags flying from the boat spelled out Harvey's name. That touched me.

I boarded Bob's boat with relatives and Harvey's friends and we prepared to head out of Newport Harbor to pass the three mile mark into International waters. We would raise no sails on this trip. We motored all the way.

His sailing friends moved around the boat with ease. Those who didn't share his passion for sailing, but loved to cycle or shoot with him, found a place to sit as soon as they boarded and remained in that place for the entire trip. I greeted them first, aware of their discomfort. I wanted them to feel as comfortable as possible, because I knew it was hard for them, and I truly appreciated that they had overcome their uneasiness in order to attend this last 'goodbye'.

As I neared Marshall and Nancy, Nancy stood up and began to tell me how sorry she was that she hadn't taken my call that night – the night I called to tell Marshall that Harvey had just passed away.

* * * *

On the night Harvey died, I drove the few blocks home from the hospital, alone, and entered the house, alone. He would never walk through those doors again.

I called the girls, my mother and my brother first. They had all been kept in the communication loop since we had first set out for the hospital at 9:00 p.m. that evening. Then, even though it was about 2:00 a.m., I began to call his family and his best friends. His friend, Dave, was first. He was shocked and saddened. When I called Marshall, he was the last of the immediate calls. I could call others in a few hours.

Marshall's wife, Nancy, answered the phone. She was irritated at the timing of the call. I told her who I was and asked for Marshall. She left the line and I waited. It was awhile before I realized she hadn't gone to bring Marshall to the phone. She just left. I hung up. I knew that Dave would call Marshall the next day. I was just sorry that I hadn't been able to tell him because Harvey loved him so much.

* * * *

Nancy was uncomfortable on the boat, standing up on the boat and feeling that she had to apologize. This was certainly not the time or the place, and the last thing I wanted was her discomfort. I tried to let her know it was alright. When something as harsh as death enters your world, a small misunderstanding becomes meaningless. It is hard for others to understand how much your world has changed and how little the small things in life matter to you.

As we moved away from shore, I moved to greet others who were there to see my husband off. Many of them had brought flowers to throw onto our ocean destination when we arrived. What a thoughtful thing to do. Harvey, or Duke, as he was known by his friends, had gathered so many warm and loyal friends.

Over the loud speaker in the pilot house we heard Dave's voice, "Whale breeching at 12 o'clock." I wanted to see this excitement charged moment, I didn't think I could move forward in time. Surely the whale would splash down before I could get there. I decided to try and moved along the side of the boat anyway, with no expectations of actually catching this momentous phenomenon.

I was so surprised to see the whale still breeched straight ahead of us. And it stayed that way; as if it was our guide. We kept on our path towards it and it continued to hold its position. Then, from the port side, moving across the front of the bow to the starboard side was a pod of dolphins so long and so deep – they swam, skipped, and dived across our path. It was like a giant dance of joy.

When we passed the three mile mark Dave cut the engines. As the piper played 'Amazing Grace' and 'Coming Home', Harvey's ashes were spread on the water at the side of the boat. A small shark appeared, his body curled into a circle as he rested next to the boat on the surface of the water. The ashes had begun to sink with the white rose petals and the bouquets of flowers marking the spot. He was completely still, and stayed there, in that spot right next to us, for the duration of our ceremony of delivering Harvey's ashes to his beloved ocean. It was as if those who lived in the ocean, the whale, the porpoises and the little shark, were there to receive his ashes with the same love, we on land delivered them. I knew he was in safe keeping.

Dave started the engine quietly, to not disturb the area or the mood. As we began to slowly move away, I heard a splash. When I looked over the side of the boat the little shark flicked the water so slightly with his tail as he uncurled his body from the circle he had held to on the surface, and then quietly slipped down, down and further down under the water.

I knew, as I watched the shark settle back into a more comfortable place for him, a place deep in the ocean, that I had found the reason for the serenity of that day…the earth and the sky, the surface of the ocean, everything above the water peaked in perfection, as it waited for us to pay our final respects and show our love to Harvey. I hadn't known until that moment that all that exists below the ocean was also in tune with our mission.

Hazel Fuller

Gerrards Market and S&H Green Stamps

In April 2019, the prompt "object" was given by Mae Wagner, the Creative Writing Workshop facilitator at the Joslyn Joy Writers Workshop in Redlands. We were to choose an object, write about it, then bring the object to the next workshop and read our story. The object I chose was a 1970 Appointment Book and Calendar from Gerrards Market, a local independent grocery store in Redlands. The first Gerrards Market opened in 1949, at 333 Orange Street. When it outgrew that space in 1966, a new store was built at the corner of Cypress and Center Street and is still serving the community. Back in the day Gerrards gave S&H Green Stamps to customers.

During the 1930s through the 1980s many department stores, grocery stores, gas stations and other retailers gave S&H stamps to customers. Founded by The Sperry & Hutchinson Company in 1896, stamps were sold to merchants and given to customers to promote loyalty and as bonuses based on the dollar amount of a purchase, one stamp for every dollar spent. Stamps were given to the customer at the checkout counter after their purchase was totaled. I remember those "lick 'em and stick 'em" stamps. My sisters and I would lick and stick stamps in a S&H Green Stamp book containing 24 pages, each page requiring 50 stamps, each book worth 1,200 points. When books were full we'd go with Mother to the local Green Stamp Redemption Store and exchange the books for merchandise or order items from the S&H Stamp Catalog.

Mother saved her books until she had enough points to exchange for a kitchen clock, dishes or other items she wanted. Many brides received china, silverware, crystal and other beautiful expensive wedding presents. Mother exchanged her books for a . . . are you ready for this? A white wicker clothes hamper that she gave me as a wedding present in 1955. Sixty five years later I still have that hamper. A very practical gift!

I started saving S&H Green Stamps after I got married. In 1960, I redeemed my books for a Boston rocker to rock my baby daughter, and later, another Boston rocker to rock my son. I thought each child would take their chair to rock their babies. They didn't. Both chairs are on my front porch where I often sit rocking, visiting with friends, neighbors and family.

The 1970 Appointment Book and Calendar I wrote about advertises S&H Green Stamps and has printed recipes. I don't know how I acquired it or who made the notations in it. I found it in a stack of recipe books I had in my pantry. The front cover shows items available when you "redeemed" your books of S&H green stamps. The last page shows merchandise available at Green Stamp Redemption Stores or through the S&H Idea Book catalog. The back cover states "The finest merchants in town give S&H green stamps!" Gerrards included twelve coupons, one for each month, "that will give the customer 100 stamps on purchases of $5.00 or more."

The month of February has a recipe for beef curry on rice and May a recipe for meat loaf. Oh, the memories of home-cooked meals with family. There are no handwritten notations until September 5th when she wrote, "started to work for Community Hospital" and on the 13th, "started taking care of Deb" and on the 29th she notes, "paid up 'til 1st for babysitting." In October she records hours worked and days off, and on the 28th she had an appointment with Dr. Brown. December 26th she wrote, "My Birthday" and the number 16. On the 27th she reminds herself that "Roller Derby starts."

My inquiring mind wants to know what happened to S&H Green Stamps? How did I come to have this 1970 Appointment Book and Calendar from Gerrards? Who had it before me? Did she work at Redlands Community Hospital or another? If she was 16 years old in 1970 she would now be 66 years old. I wonder who she is and where she is today. I wonder what happened to Roller Derby.

That "object" prompt took me on a sentimental journey reminiscing about S&H Green Stamps, Gerrards Market, my Mother, my wicker hamper and my Boston rockers. The journey left me wondering to whom that 1970 Appointment Book and Calendar belonged? I wonder if she would enjoy seeing it and reminiscing about her life fifty years ago.

Hazel Fuller

Miss Curry's Typing Class

Miss Curry's typing class was in room 202 located on the second floor of the Fine Arts Building at the Redlands High School on Citrus Avenue in Redlands, California. Founded in 1891, the school's main building was expanded over the years and new buildings appeared including the Household Arts Building, later renamed the Fine Arts Building. Home economic and business classes, as well as art classes were located in the Fine Arts Building.

Miss Curry was teaching at RHS in the 1930s when she taught typing to my oldest sister many years before I was a student in the 1950s. She was probably in her fifties which seemed very old to me as a fifteen year old. Her short gray hair, parted on one side, was permed into finger waves. She wore stylish dresses or two piece suits made of silk, cotton, rayon or wool. Some dresses had lace collars and cuffs and buttons or buckles as fasteners. The hems of her clothes hit mid- calf and she wore classic, modest heeled shoes, dark colored oxfords, or lace-ups that tied in a small bow. Female teachers did not wear trousers in the 1950s. She was a no-nonsense teacher. We entered the classroom, sat at our desk and as soon as the bell rang she began the day's lesson.

Room 202 was a large room with high ceilings, double hung windows on the east wall, the sun filling the room with natural light. To me, it was a beautiful room with oak floors, beautiful light fixtures hanging from the ceiling, heavy oak doors with brass door knobs and opaque windows. Thirty or more oak tables, each with an oak chair, stood in rows. A Royal or Underwood typewriter was on each desk, along with a blue hard covered Beginners Typing Manual. Each typewriter had a cover "to keep the typewriter clean," according to Miss Curry. We removed it when we sat down to type and replaced it before leaving the classroom. A blackboard was on the front wall with white chalk and felt erasers on the tray at the bottom of the board. A tall wind-up Victrola phonograph in an oak cabinet stood in the front right hand corner near the blackboard.

At the beginning of each period Miss Curry would stand in front of the class. "Open your manual to page one," she would say. We learned the parts of a typewriter. We learned how to roll typing paper into the roller mechanism. We learned how to place our fingers on the keys, how to strike the key firmly. "Today we will practice the letters a, s, d, f, and j, k, l, and the semi colon" she would say. "With a one, and a two" count we would strike the appropriate key as she called out each letter. Letter by letter we learned the keyboard, practice after practice learned touch typing. We learned how to insert the black/red ribbon, black on the bottom, red on the top, and how to reverse the ribbon when it reached the end of the spool. We learned how to tabulate data and how to use that dreaded carbon paper.

Timed tests increased our speed and we practiced these little ditties to increase speed: "All work and no play makes Jack a dull boy." And this one: "The quick brown fox jumps over the lazy dog," This sentence contains all letters of the alphabet.

Miss Curry had a collection of 78 RPM records she played on the Victrola phonograph while we typed. As we placed fingers on the keyboard, Miss Curry hurried across the room to the Victrola, placed a record on the turntable, cranked the handle to wind up the Victrola, set the needle on the record and the music began. We stuck the a, and the s, and the d, and the f, with our left hand fingers and the j, and the k, and the l, and the ; with our right hand fingers. We typed to the tune of "The Toreador Song" from the opera "Carmen" or the beat of "Semper Fidelis" or "The William Tell Overture" or another of John Phillip Sousa's marches. As the record played and we typed Miss Curry walked around the room with a wooden ruler in her right hand slapping the palm of her left hand keeping time with the music. As she called out a letter we were to strike the key to the beat of the music and the slap of the ruler. As the Victrola wound down so did our typing speed until Miss Curry cranked it up again and our fingers moved fast once more. Although my typing speed was never great, the skills I learned in Miss Curry's typing class have served me well over the past seventy years.

Oh, Miss Curry, you'd be amazed at today's technology! Your Victrola phonograph, your wonderful 78 RPM record collection, your Royals, your Underwoods – now museum pieces! Computers have replaced typewriters and much more. What cannot be replaced are my memories of the sounds of typewriters in room 202 of the Fine Arts Building in the early 1950s. The "tap, tap, tap" as the letters struck the paper, the "ding" of the carriage return bell, the "zzzzzzip" when pulling the paper out of the roller mechanism. I remember entering the Fine Arts Building, turning right in the hall, climbing the stairs to the second floor, turning right again toward room 202 and hearing the sound of woodpeckers, tap, tap, tap as I walked down the hall to my typing class.

The typewriters are gone, the Fine Arts Building gone, Manual Arts Building gone, Administration Building gone. All demolished in the 1960s. "Unsafe" they said, "because they were not earthquake proof," replaced by "temporary" classrooms built in the sixties, still there sixty years later. The Clock Auditorium, library and girls gym are the only buildings remaining on the campus where you taught. No beautiful ivy covered Administration Building, or Fine Arts Building, no room 202. But on this computer keyboard I am using, my fingers tap easily and quickly, selecting letters, forming words, "touch typing" faster than I could on a typewriter, all the while I reminisce about Miss Curry's typing class in room 202 in the Fine Arts Building at the Redlands High School on Citrus Avenue in Redlands, California.

RICHARD HESS

She Fooled Me Again

This is a story about me and my two children. At the time of this story my daughter Carrie was 9 and my son Brian was seven. Brian was recovering from a viral illness – slight fever, nausea, generally not feeling well. He had missed school for 3 days. But now he was over it. He was running around, happy, full of energy.

Then Carrie said, "Dad, I will make you a bet that Brian stays home from school tomorrow. Ten bucks." I took this bet because I thought there was no way I could lose. Brian looked perfectly healthy. Obviously, I would not take her money, just have the great satisfaction of winning the bet. Because even at age nine my daughter had a remarkable ability to trick me and fool me.

Well, the next morning I came into the living room. Brian was there and he looked great!! I thought "Surely he is going to school today." Then Carrie came in and spoke in a very concerned voice. "Brian how do you feel? You look really pale. Is your tummy upset? Do you feel like you might throw up? Are your muscles weak and achy? Let me check your forehead. Oh, you feel hot. I think you might have a fever!" You should go sit down and rest. Carrie then told Mom, "Brian is not feeling well. He is sick. I think he needs to stay home from school today."

Mom asked Brian how he felt, and he said he felt kinda weak and sick. Mom decided he should stay home. I protested this decision citing the lack of a demonstrated fever, i.e. temperature of 100.4 degrees or higher. But this was to no avail. In such matters Mom's decision is final. Bottom line – Brian stayed home from school, Carrie won the bet and my 10 dollars. And Brian was happy because he really didn't want to go to school anyway. The only loser was me.

This made me realize that this is what we often do to ourselves. We get up in the morning and think," I'm tired, I didn't sleep well. I have no energy. I look in the mirror and see my tired, bloodshot eyes. I think, "When I feel like this, I usually get a headache – yes, there is one starting. And usually my back starts hurting – ok I feel that sacroiliac pain now. Surely, I will have a lousy day. Everyone will be difficult and annoying. So, my whole day will be a nightmare – and probably the rest of the week as well.

Well, what should we do? If we have a pain – ok we do, but don't generalize to everything else. Don't exaggerate or 'catastrophize'. Counter negative thoughts with positive ones which are more accurate about what is really going on.

Be thankful for what you do have. I am alive and most body parts are still working – kindof. And the pain is minimal, especially if I think about something positive, like my amazing beautiful 19-month-old granddaughters. Life is good!

RICHARD HESS

First Date

    Unbelievable! I asked her out and she said "Yes"! As background I am an OBGYN doctor and I had joined a medical group in Fairbanks, Alaska two years earlier. I was extremely busy as I was one of only two OB docs in the group. I had always felt the Lord would lead me to someone and we would have a lovely family. Only problem – there were very few single, unattached women there in Fairbanks. It seemed that all the attractive women were either married or in relationships. I had found a nice church, but folks there were either elderly or teenagers. I was beginning to feel hopeless. I thought I would be more likely to find Bigfoot than a wife! Then, one day I was making rounds in the hospital and I saw a nurse who was new and very attractive. Marie had come from Missouri to continue her nursing studies at the University of Alaska. However, the U of A Nursing Program was in Anchorage, not Fairbanks. A lucky mistake, Marie coming to Fairbanks. I asked her out but she said she was going back to Missouri where her family lived. Bummer! I had finally found this really nice girl and now she was leaving before I got a chance to know her!

    Well guess what? When she flew out she got a strong feeling that she should return to Fairbanks. Thank you, Jesus! So I asked her out for a date. I thought this was too good to be true and she would find some polite way to say no. But - she said she would love to go out with me! Our first date was at a very nice restaurant, "Club 11", which was 11 miles on the road from Fairbanks to North Pole, Alaska. We had lobster that evening, and we found out that we shared many of the same values and opinions about life. I knew I had found the one for me.

    The main obstacle for me to overcome was that she really did not want to marry a doctor. She said she used to babysit, and doctors' kids were often the worst, spoiled-rotten little monsters and she did not want that. However, perhaps against her better judgment, she married me. And that was 43 years ago. I am sure there were times she would have liked to whack me in the head and throw me into the Chena River. But, as you can see, that never happened. If she had not married me heaven knows what would have happened. There is one poor elderly guy who keeps putting ads in the local paper trying to find a date. I guess that would have been me! Rich Hess

Rosalie Hruska

Someday

    Someday, I'll be over you. Someday, I won't wake hoping that today I'll hear from you. Someday my head won't be filled with thoughts of you, remembering what you said and did and how your eyes smiled when they looked into mine. Someday I will forget how happy I felt when we were together. Someday I will eat your favorite foods and not think of you. Someday I will fall asleep without thinking of you - of where you are or who you are with. Someday I will not glance at my phone to see if you called. Someday I will forget about you like you forgot about me. Just not today---but someday

GARY NEUHARTH

Abstract Grace

Cold wind blows in Rockland and its cold love from the rich.
Its hard knuckles and callused hands
    that shape the beauty of love in "richland" and no one shows emotion.
They all listen to the music and the wild bird flies inside their heads.
    It's a rare and beautiful bird playing over and over inside their heads.
They let it fly free and it's there as long as they want it to be.
    Others are caught up in the soulful spirit's wind.
They think they must have this bird,
    but their own greed suffocates beauty's bird
    and the profound moment quickly evaporates
    and the moment is desolation
    and the music is forgotten,
    as the inspiration of the moment quickly fades away.
The pretty people carry themselves with Aryan grace,
    curiously resembling celestial bird cages,
    as they walk about caught up in the sweep of the melody,
    and although no one chooses to claim understanding of abstract grace
    they're caught up in the moment, and they're caught up in pace
    and nobody seems to wonder how they'll catch up in this race.
"Richland" throws back its head while wearing a new neck brace
    They plot how they can nail you and get down on your case.
The rare bird flies through an empty hall and feels comfortable in its place.
Don't worry about your clothes now or worry about your face –
    just step inside and take a ride to the music of abstract grace.

Gary Neuharth

Lord Of The Rails

It was night and he was under a street light at the edge of the city. The serenity in his eyes was like the cries of children in the wind and I, in my eagerness, took him in. He was a curious person in my world. I walked with him to my gathering place – he reveled in the atmosphere; it was as if time had turned backwards for him. It was a place for poets, and since there were no readers that damp night, he began to speak. He spoke of hills and valleys and mountain tops, of meadows and high waving grass, of camps for riders by the tracks. He always came back to the tracks and the people huddled over fires with the rain on their backs. He forgot, as his gratitude gleamed and his voice filled the room like an electric beam. Dark figures came in and invaded his dream and took him outside to interrogate him, and there he stood. He'd been here before. They told him to leave and come back no more. So I took him outside, to the edge of town. As I wrote in my book about the freeway, the serenity slid from his face.

He pulled a flask from his jeans
   and offered me a place in his race,
   derided my poems,
   and commanded me to follow him to the tracks
   to some friends he knew
   to sleep for the night in the cold and dew,
   and eat from a can by an open fire
   alone and awake in a desolate place.
He wasn't smiling anymore
   and each time I spoke he screamed at me.
   "You think you can write about this place
   and go back to your bed in a comfortable place

or write in your pad in flowery words.
Tonight you will know about this place
   for you'll sleep on the rocks and feel the cold.
You won't be so noble and you won't be so bold.
You'll feel the hunger and you'll feel very old
   and you'll lose your freedom and do what you're told."
The free soul I had met disappeared
   and stood mocking me with an obvious leer.
"You don't know me, but from now on,
   when you hear the train's whistle
   you'll lower your head in newfound respect, for I've shown you
   my way and how I step on a moonless night."
I left that night, cold and wet
   While the Lord of the Rails sat down and wept.

Gary Neuharth

Road Trip

I stand in the middle of the earth, at the core, wanting more to explore.

Mo thy car Mama
Cleveland, the capital of sensibility is awakened

Much more I say
And it comes to me, without measure, bountifully

What about

The others, on their search,
looking for the illusive icon two steps to the right and you're back on 14th street in the
   bi-partisan parade
looking for the steps to follow to Belleview – watch out for that elephant.

Welcome to the jungle. Welcome to the humble. Welcome bowing to the proud.
Welcome to the church yard with angels dressed in shrouds.
Rocks lying on the ground
   black, white, yellow and brown.
Big, little, likely and profound.
Light, bright, inside take a ride.
Say "Hello" to your body, your mind and your kind.
To thy own self, the human machine.
First, after all, no more family barbecues.
Ethnic divisions and protestant multilevel networks, forced.

No more pay toilets, toll booths, red light sales by stop signs or urban Nazis standing by telephone soldiers selling software artillery non-stop.

Sold on me is no longer a hostage to confidence men side-stepping the issue and the little dog who thought you were a tree and those standing in the meadow waiting for the sun to come up and the grass to grow.

And the Nun in the stock market hailing a cab or the choirboy with a suitcase at the edge and the clowns at the airport looking for love.

I remember Bromberger's Shoes twelve miles from Cleveland by the Fairfield Exit with eleven girls from Singapore in drag on a Saturday night on Angel's Flight just short of New Haven shouting, "Go up, man".

I remember Walt Whitman through the Hollenbeck tunnel at noonday when I was three cents short of a dollar.

I was surprised when the man with the pitchfork waved at me by the side of the road just outside of Connecticut with an ecstatic five gallon bucket.

I remember the piccolo player with the mouse in his pocket, elated while children danced by the water's edge on a summer afternoon while overnight hat holders expressed themselves in a singular way to the Bishop.

Gary Neuharth

Stealer of Dreams

I did not recognize it at first
The wagging head
And the shaking finger
The hands on the hips and the Bible beater
The words rushed out
You'll do what's proper
And you'll do what's right
You'll not dream aloud
Or imagine things
You'll follow the rules
And ask no questions
This is the way it has been
And the way it will always be
You'll respect the elders
With no respect returned
You'll not dawdle, nor daydream
You'll walk straight
And hold your head in the proper posture
You'll do what you've been told
And not be too bold
You'll walk down the middle road
And not stray to your right or left
I became aware of this curious creature
The preacher teacher
It was not the first time
And it had many faces

It stole the sky and the beauty of freedom
It criticized love and imagination
It patrolled the streets
And the lobbies of churches
Turned bright colors into dreary grayness
Scolded playing children
And changed the music to a stiffened marching song
The bigot, the critic
I had not recognized it at first
But now it became all too familiar
It was the stealer of dreams and nothing more

Gary Neuharth

Vampire Queen

Better watch out, better watch out, for the Vampire Queen
She's warm, she's pretty, she's cool, she's mean
You shake, you shimmy, you burn like coals
Better watch out for the Vampire Queen

She walks so stately, followed by her train
She smiles, she gleams, she's so serene
And if she don't like you, vampire watcher
All you get is an ethereal gleam

When she arrives, that is the scene
If you're around you're in the dream
She's tall, she's skinny and just prime lean
Her heart beats like a sewing machine

High and lofty, full of fire, she waits in darkness, eyes of flame
Playing a proud and hateful game
Better watch out, for the Vampire Queen

One hard look and she'll make you scream
Tiny coffins, pickled people, empty chairs
All part of the world of the Vampire Queen

Red-rich red, bed head, bled dead
She flies into the room bathed in steam
Only to be equaled by prostrate bows

She's lean, she's pretty, she's kind of mean
Turn your head and she's gone like a dream
So you better watch out, boy, better watch it!

Don't look too long or she'll drain you dry and watch you die
So you better watch out for her, she'll get you, she'll get you
That Vampire Queen

KRISTINE ANN SHELL

The Wind

It's just the wind
and nothing more,
whispering in the grass,
whistling through the trees,
kicking up the dirt,
rolling in the leaves,
scratching on my walls,
clawing at the screens,
tearing at my roof,
pounding on the eaves,
running up my steps,
raging at my door,
It's just the wind
and nothing more.

On My Way Home

I was driving home early Wednesday afternoon with our oldest son, Morgan, in the passenger seat next to me. I'd left work right before lunch to pick Morgan up from school. The secretary at Cajon High School had called to say Morgan had sat on a wad of gum at lunch, and he wanted to go home. Morgan's a senior at Cajon, a good student who rarely misses a day of school, so I was happy to pick him up and save him the embarrassment of returning to class. Ryan, Morgan's younger brother also goes to Cajon, He's two years younger than Morgan and more interested in fast food and video games than his classes. Our home is walking distance from Cajon High School and just past the Cal State University campus.

Morgan was seated in the passenger seat next to me, complaining on and on about the wad of gum that had stuck itself to his dockers. I was letting him vent, half listening, when Morgan abruptly stopped his venting and shouted, "Wait! Who's that?"

Morgan was pointing to a young man with his back to us walking along the road towards Cal State. I slowed my car, stared at the young man, and did a double take. Was that Ryan?

I pulled to the side of the road as Morgan lowered the passenger side window.

"Ryan!" Morgan shouted.

Morgan turned to me as I brought my car to a stop and set the brake. He was grinning widely.

"This ought to be good!" he said.

"Where ya' going?" Morgan shouted as he stepped out of the car.

Ryan stopped and turned to face his older brother. He had

that 'deer in the headlights' look – frozen in his tracks, eyes wide open.

A dozen questions filled my head. What was Ryan doing? Why wasn't he in school?

"What's going on?" I asked Ryan. "Why aren't you at school?"

"I'm on my way to the library," Ryan answered.

Morgan laughed. "Wrong direction!" he said as he pointed toward Cajon High School.

\

"Not the Cajon library," Ryan said, "the Cal State library. Cajon's library doesn't have the book I need for my report. So, I got a library pass, and I'm headed to the Cal State library."

I stared at Ryan. I wasn't buying it. "Where's your pass?" I asked.

"My pass?" Ryan answered. "It's here somewhere." Ryan made a half-hearted attempt to search the pockets of his jeans.

Morgan was still grinning. "You are in so much trouble!"

Ryan continued to search for his pass. He was fumbling through his backpack.

"I must have lost it," he said.

"You were going to Cal State's Hub to play videogames!" Morgan said.

I glared at Ryan. Did he really think I was buying his story?

"Get in the car," I told Ryan.

I followed both boys as they headed to the car.

Then, Ryan paused to look back at me.

"What about my report?" he asked.

"Don't you dare say another word," I told Ryan.

**ONTARIO AT
THE ONTARIO PUBLIC LIBRARY**

with Tim Hatch

Tim Hatch

PCH Sunset (New Year's Day, 2016)

Sydney pants in the sand before us, all
ran out. Annette's phone mimics a shutter
as she tries to capture the sky. I lean

back on a massive, tan rock, smooth
and pitted with burrows from a thousand
generations of Angelwing clams. Between

competing sounds of ocean and highway, my eyes
tilt up toward the light, closed, and I
listen to the sunset. I used to live a block

north of the 10, and I used to think, at night
that the endless stream of traffic sounded like
a river. Behind us, I hear only traffic.

If a freeway is a river it's a deformed
mechanical thing. No fish. No pulse. Get
close to an actual river, you can hear

the life inside, the steady whisper of water
on the shore. The ocean before us sounds
like the wind if the wind had a plan or patience enough

to see it through, and the shoreline pulses softly
with creation song, stories of lost
gods, dreams of plankton, nameless unseen.

Tim Hatch

Oedipal Revenge Fantasy

Standing up from the dinner table, my father asks when
I plan on fixing the dent in my truck. *You know*, he says,
when I was your age—

"You know what, dad? When Jesus was your age he'd been
dead for forty years. All of us fail
to measure up to someone."

Yeah, well, at least I wasn't living off my wife.

A flash of blood and I'm outside
myself. The dinner table falls from under me,
followed quickly by the Earth, the solar system,
and the galaxy. Alone, drifting, formless, and so,
so quiet.
I see red dwarfs and nebulous clouds and the colors, dear God,
the colors. The pinks and blues and yellows and the blinding,
piercing white. Slowly it dawns
on me that I'm not in the universe so much as

I am the universe – the same
perfect recipe of hydrogen, oxygen, carbon, and nitrogen
as everything else – and I am fucking gorgeous. And huge.

Singing begins, sublime,
glorious, my creation
song, in flawless harmony with myself,
trumpets on a clear, still morning.

All human knowledge, everything
we've ever known, enough data
to destroy a mind,
doesn't add up to a single star in the sky, not even

the memory of a star.

My pride, my ego, my father's
arrogance and disapproval…meaningless.
That I'd allow any one person to define
my life is an act of hubris

so great as to defy sanity.
I cannot hate my father for the simple fact that I am
my father. And he is me and we
are every mosquito flitting
on the surface of every river on every world. And this

sends me home,
and I fall   home   back
to the dinner table   back   in my body
and you know what? He's still a fucking asshole. So
I curl my hand into a fist   a fist   a universe
unto itself, and I sink to my knees
and I punch him in the cock.

The Boy Who Could Fly

Once there was a boy who could fly.

He discovered it one sunny, summer day when playing with his best friend on a bridge near their homes. Their parents warned them not to play there, but that's what made it so fun. Daring each other to take bigger chances, the friend pressured the boy to climb and walk along the railing. He mounted and spread his arms as if he were on a high wire.

A fast-moving van brushed close, kicking up a strong breeze.

The friend reached out to stabilize the boy, but acted too slowly to stop the fall.

Dropping toward the rock-laden river below in slow motion, the boy had time to consider his inevitable death or, worse, his severe pain and possible disability or disfigurement.

Time slowed further as the boy breezed through things he'd hoped to do with his life. He wondered why this was happening and if he could stop it… somehow. He couldn't let go like this.

In the last seconds, he bore down on his determination, certain he could save himself.

Ten feet above the river, he slowed and a foot above, he stopped over the raging water.

Muscles tensed, he held himself steady and took a deep breath, amazed. Then he shot up into the sky, like a bullet or jet, spinning slowly as he soared.

He flew past the bridge, briefly glimpsing his friend, eyes wide and mouth hanging open.

In the days that followed, the boy learned to do barrel rolls and high-speed dives he'd pull out of at the last moment. He liked to fly low over water, skimming the surface, creating perfect waves in his wake. But most of all, he liked performing aerial maneuvers in crowded urban streets where he'd make a perfect landing to the applause of strangers.

Then he woke up…

And learned he was not a boy. He was a lonely, middle-aged man, with a bulging belly and debt that would haunt him for the rest of his life. His dead-end job would never provide enough for him to move from the dirty city where he lived in a rundown apartment in a bad part of town.

When he was younger, he hoped he might win the love of a woman, but he'd always been unattractive—maybe downright ugly—so he had no experience with romance.

He worked in a call center with a cluster of unpleasant, faceless men and women who had no interest in friendships at work because they had enough problems at home. Every time he tried to start a conversation, they'd shoot him down, making him feel worse than before.

The height of his social experience was having coffee with the priest at the church a few blocks from where he lived. They'd met in a diner and randomly struck up a conversation. Although the man was not Catholic and uncertain of his exact beliefs, he respected the priest. A friendship was born.

They'd meet after Mass on Sundays in the rectory. The man couldn't remember the priest's name. If he'd ever known it, he'd forgotten, and thought it would be rude to ask now. He simply called the man Father, since that's what everyone else seemed to call him. Even though the man was not religious, he enjoyed talking with the priest and considered him a friend—his only friend.

"Did you have one of those dreams again?" asked the priest.

"Yes, like every other night."

"I've heard flight dreams sometimes come to those with a powerful desire to escape."

"Escape? What do I have to escape from, Father?"

"You're always telling me how you hate your life—where you live, what you do, your prospects for the future."

"I suppose. But all my dreams are different since the accident."

"Thank God the fall didn't kill you," said the priest. "What were you doing on your roof, anyway?"

"Adjusting the TV antenna. I refuse to pay one of those carnivorous cable companies."

The pastor smiled. "I'm just glad you're alright."

"Me, too, I think."

NIGHT

Now that he could fly, cute girls from down the street finally noticed him. They gathered at his house after school, to watch him do flying tricks. He put on performances in his front yard until a few distracted drivers crashed their cars. His parents made him move his show to the backyard.

Occasionally, he'd fly a pretty girl home from school. It seemed all of them wanted a ride in the sky. For the first time in his life, the boy was popular.

He happily gave rides to girls who wanted them. When jealous boyfriends cornered him, he listened to their threats for a while. When it looked like they might get violent, he simply flew away.

DAY

The clergyman poured warm tea for his friend. "You were saying?"

"Thank you." The man drank deep. "Lately, I've been uncertain which is the dream and which is reality."

The priest's eyebrows furrowed. "Huh?"

"My dreams are so crystal clear lately. And I have more control than ever before. It's like I'm most awake when I'm dreaming. This life is the one I loathe returning to. It's a nightmare, compared to the wondrous world I experience when I'm sleeping."

"This isn't such a terrible life," said the priest. "Is it? You have a place to live, food to eat, relatively good health, and an exceedingly wise and handsome priest who serves you tea and listens. But seriously, many pray for those basic things you take for granted."

"You're right. I should be grateful. But I know in my gut, I am supposed to fly, like I was born to it. So, anything less depresses me."

The priest scratched his head. "How could someone be born to something like that?"

The man went silent, then said, "If things were different, it might be something humans do, like swimming or running."

"Seriously?"

"Yes," said the man. "What if we could run an experiment where we raised a child in the belief that everyone flies? And, using illusions of some kind, made a convincing case for it?"

"You're suggesting the boy would be able to fly because that would be the only reality he knows?"

"Yes, Father. There are many examples of humans being unable to do things until one person found a way. After that, it wasn't nearly as difficult to imagine everyone doing it."

"Like the first person to ride a bicycle?"

"That's not exactly what I meant. Maybe it's more like the first flying machines. There were many of them that failed. Then, eventually, we crossed that boundary. Now, building a glider would be almost intuitive. Not that it would work every time, but you and I would stand a decent chance of building a functional flying machine if we tried. It would be that much easier, knowing it was possible."

"We could?" asked the priest.

"No, not us specifically. I meant average people could do it. The first time we walk a certain mile, the journey might seem long. Then, after that, it feels shorter because we know the road better than we did the first time. I believe it's the same way with knowledge."

"But flight without feathers?"

"Bats don't have feathers, Father."

"Okay. Flight without *wings*?"

"Weren't several of your saints supposed to be able to fly?"

Under his breath the priest said, "Saint Joseph of Cupertino, among others."

"See."

"Tell me, are you a saint now?" The priest grinned.

"No. I only meant that even religions acknowledge it's possible. Hinduism also tells of famous yogis levitating?"

"Are we talking about levitation or actual flight?"

"In my case, Father, it's real flight, not just up and down. It's like I'm one of those superheroes."

NIGHT

The building collapsed in pieces around the terrified mother and her babe as flames raged closer. Just when all seemed lost, the boy swooped in and picked up the woman and her child and flew them to safety…

The mugger ran down the street, easily outpacing the elderly woman whose purse he'd grabbed. Just when it seemed he would get away, the boy landed on him hard, bringing down the crook. The lady had tears on her face as she kissed him on the cheek and told him she thought he was a sweet boy…

The single father grew desperate when his two children ran off and became lost in the woods. Despite attempts by police, forest rangers and volunteers, the kids could not be found. However, able to rise above the trees, the flying boy could see much farther than those on the ground. He located the children and flew them back to a grateful father.

DAY

"Have you noticed how similar your real-life accident falling from your roof and your dream accident, falling from a bridge are?"

"No, I didn't notice. What's your point?"

"I think your dream life seems so realistic to you because of that parallel. You don't really believe you can fly in real life? Do you?"

"Actually, I'm beginning to think I can."

"You're not considering jumping from some height, cause that's just suicide? Couldn't you try taking off from the ground first?"

"No, I think near perfect faith may be necessary to do it."

"You can't find that faith a little closer to Earth?"

"No, I don't think I can. All my life, it's been drilled into me that flying under our own power is impossible. To overcome that, I think I must face the threat of death."

"That's crazy. You know, the Bible teaches suicide is a sin."

"You forget. I believe in God and heaven and the angels and all that, but I am not a member of your faith or your flock."

"Yes, I always forget that. You seem like such a spiritual person to me, our long talks and all. Maybe I was mistaking philosophy for faith. Either way, this is a horrible idea. I don't want you to die over some silly notion you picked up in a dream."

The man frowned at the priest.

"Look," said the priest, "if people were capable of flight, don't you think, for the billions of people on this planet, we would have heard of such a thing by now?"

"Unless governments snatched them off the streets and kept them in black sites."

The priest chuckled. "Where they could dissect and experiment on them?"

The man mumbled, "Maybe."

"Come on. A conspiracy theory? Really?"

"Father, I'm meant to do this."

The priest shook his head. "I don't know."

The man wondered why his only friend, a clergyman, could not understand this was a serious calling. He left without saying goodbye.

NIGHT

The late-night talk show host grinned and shook the boy's

hand. "Thank you for coming to see us. But it's a little past your bedtime, isn't it?"

The crowd laughed.

The boy smirked and took a seat.

"I understand you can actually fly," said the host.

"Yes, I can."

"How do you do that?"

The boy paused like he was preparing to explain, then blurted out, "I don't know."

The crowd roared.

The host faced the camera, grinning. "I have my doubts but, as they say, seeing is believing. Can you show us?"

"Sure." The boy stood and rose into the air, then zoomed over the applauding audience, exploring the spacious studio auditorium.

DAY

"I'm going to do it next Sunday. I'll wait until you finish your service duties at the church."

"What are you going to do?" asked the priest.

"Fly, of course. I want you to be there."

"Please don't attempt that. It's impossible. Suicide. Your life may not be everything you want, but that's no excuse to throw it away."

"I'm not, Father. I can do this."

The following Sunday, the priest met his friend at a downtown building and followed him up several flights of stairs to the roof. "Please don't go out there. It's not a good idea."

After receiving no response, the clergyman said, "Stop a second. I have something I need to say before you do this."

The man halted in his tracks and sagged in place. "What is it, now?"

"Have you ever heard of the sin of presumption?"

"No, I don't think so."

"If you plan to step off a cliff and say to yourself, 'God, save me if you're really there.' Then you jump? That's a sin—the sin of presumption."

The man sighed and shook his head. "I told you I am not a member of your religion, Father, but even if I were, I don't expect God to save me. I'll do this on my own."

"It won't work. Lately you've had problems telling the difference between your dreams and reality. In dreams, you can jump from a height and fly. In reality, you'll die. It's that simple. And it's crucial, if you can't tell the difference, that you learn how."

"I'm sorry you don't have more faith in me, Father. I'm going to prove this to you."

"I don't need proof. I just…" The priest raced ahead and barred the roof access door. "Look, I didn't want you to hurt yourself. That's why I did what I did."

The man pushed past him. "What are you talking about?"

Outside, on the roof, two policemen approached.

"What did you do?" The man shook his head, frowning.

"I called them. I'm sorry, I had to do something."

"I thought you were my friend."

The policemen escorted him from the building to their car.

NIGHT

The boy's arch enemy trapped him in a steel cage. "Now you'll never get away. You'll never fly again."

For a moment, the boy wasn't sure how he'd escape. Then he realized, besides the ability to fly, he had super strength. Or maybe he'd made that so, by willing it. Whatever the cause, he burst free of the cage, grabbed the stolen government secrets and leaped into the air, making his getaway.

The villain fired an energy beam from a strange-looking alien weapon.

One blast knocked the boy to the ground where he lay very

still.

The villain cackled until he saw the boy sit up and shake off the beam's effect.

"You can't stop me from flying. Nobody can."

DAY

The man waited where he'd climbed near the top of the church steeple. Although he hadn't given warning this time, he knew the priest would arrive soon. The clergyman had turned him in, a few weeks earlier, but the man believed the father had done that out of genuine concern. He had to prove to the priest he could really do it. He would fly that day.

A crowd gathered on the sidewalk below. Some onlookers lifted their phones to photograph him standing on the roof or to film his leap. Others, more animated, spoke into them. He felt certain they'd notified the police. He hoped the priest would arrive before they did. But the man would jump that day, whether or not his friend arrived in time.

The priest appeared in the crowd and shouted to him, "This is crazy. Don't do it!"

The man yelled back, "I can do this, Father. You'll see."

"Can't we talk about this? Please come down from there."

As the man leaned over the edge, the crowd collectively seemed to take a deep breath.

"Here I go," the man muttered.

He lifted his arms and readied himself.

A fleeting moment of doubt overtook him and, for just a second, he worried he couldn't summon the faith he'd require. But in the next second, he banished the doubt from his mind and dove fearlessly into the air. *I believe. I BELIEVE.*

POETS IN MOTION AT THE JANET GOESKE SENIOR CENTER IN RIVERSIDE

with CelenaDiana Bumpus

Poets In Motion Unity Poem 2019

Inlandia Goeske, Janet Goeske Senior Center, Riverside, Ca

CelenaDiana Bumpus, Harri-J Cardiel, Florence Lucero, Sylvia Clarke, Wil Clarke, Gudelia Vaden, Joan Jones, Phyllis Ahpuk Reis, Tom Vaden, Shirley Petro-Timura, Heather Takenaga, MaryAnn Holmes, Alan Van Tassel, Donna Slezak, Sam Barclay, Georgette Buckley, Phyllis Maynard, Aaron Craig

In Memoriam and In Honorarium

We share laughter, love and our lives
United every Tuesday
We are unequivocally family
Each of us branches of a grafted tree
Each fruit unique but still part of the whole

"United We Stand"—and so
   it begins
The long trek to freedom
   for all
And centuries later we're
   struggling still
Mankind is as stubborn as
   Hell.

In Unity I find what working with
   my classmates
   side by side is a great
   humankind
Unity consists of
   Unjudgemental

Nacent acceptance of
Individuals and their
Talents and efforts
Yesterday, today, always

Writing consumes our time
Do it in a word
Of course it has to rhyme
Even when overheard

Together we can do
what we can do
if we work together
to write a poem of love
Because what is love without
unity?

Unity fellowship of one?
No. More than one
Love our unity
Love our fellowship
We are one

I feel so blessed to be alive
for another Christmas
of seventy-three years.
I am truly blesssed
as a student for writing
poetry, fiction and nonfiction.
Thank you Celena Bumpus
for our unity

Flowing through life with help
Empathy for others and self

Concept learned, etched forever

One together joins
   to be writers
   perhaps to earn coins
But we become friends
  as sharing our skills
    that never ends

Smiles in different shapes
Litany of stories
Pulls us and ties us
In the cycle
Of trust

United in time and purpose
years of experience to share
acceptance and encouragement
a collaborative effort, fellowship and care
When Tuesday comes around—
I can always hear the sound
of Celena's voice abound.
Tuesdays ring a satisfaction
that I will meet in kindred attraction
My fellow Quillsters, not a faction.
Unity is the glue that gives
our class, a cohesive goal
of success and camaraderie.
It is what keeps our class
so vibrant.

We are all related
We come from the same
pair of genes from the beginning

And we all like to
eat each other's food
and wear jeans.

Love it...Being here
Today it's Christmas
   feel the good cheer?

There'll Wil quoting Chaucer
   and Jose with his quill
   and Delia keeping order
   as Delia will

The food's the best
   with every good taste
   the aroma is wafting
   all over this place

Like Aspen leaves flutter
On the majestic tree
In a grove so vast
As the eye can see

On separate tree
On separate branch
Together not separate
They do their leaf dance

Sam Barclay

Adventure Gone Awry

Suddenly I'm awake. But this is not my bed. Oh yes. Now I remember... Mom kissing me—I'm on the gurney, then —on the operating table, strapped down, the smell of ether, counting backwards 99, 98, 97...that's the last I heard. Until now. WOW. I'm alive. I made it. Thank you, Lord. Thank you.

This all started in Mr. Boyers Manual Arts class in the seventh grade. There I attached myself to Buddy Shepard and Dino Theodoran. We made a threesome that stuck together through junior high, into high school and well beyond. Yes, we learned the tools of the trade like a cross cut saw. And I, the ripsaw and a coping saw. We also made tables and magazine racks. Buddy made a rabbit hutch.

Together we joined the Boy Scouts and did summer camp at Lake Manitou. At night, we would sit around the campfire and sing songs like, "I've Been Working on the Railroad All the Live long Day". Then, in our tents at night, we would be saying things like; my feet are cold or was it my peter's cold?—ha, ha, ha.

In ninth grade, we were growing up. One time, we borrowed Dino's dad's model 'a Ford' and went up to that gold mining town of Cripple Creek, Colorado. On our way home, we went to restaurant in Divide, Colorado. It was a little restaurant. When we ask for a menu, that little old man said, "We have Hamburgers and Chili."

Dino asked, "What else do you have?" and got the same reply; "Hamburgers and Chili". Being smart ass kids, we taunted the old fellow repeatedly with "Hamburgers and Chili". He threatened us with a long rubber hose and made us leave. We ran to the car and yelled, "Hamburgers and Chili" laughing as we drove away.

We all decided, during Christmas vacation, we were going to go rabbit hunting. We had made all the arrangements and were set. But Buddys little brother, Bruce, told us that if we didn't take him, he would tell Mom. So he won and we borrowed a rifle for Bruce and the trip was on again.

The day came and we were out on the prairie—ten or twelve miles east of Colorado Springs. We didn't see any rabbits—probably because they heard us coming as we were shooting at imaginary targets and simply having fun. At noon, we gathered together to eat our sack lunches. I thought I saw something moving in the bushes some fifty feet away and went there to check things out. Little Bruce tagged along with me. I was bent over, looking into these bushes when a rifle shot rang out. Bruce had accidently pulled the trigger on his rifle and I was in the line of fire. I yelled out, "I've been shot!" and fell to the ground in pain. Buddy and Dino were there right away, wondering what to do. Dino realized we need to get help and ran the 200 hundred yards to that country road. He hailed down a farmer that was on his way to town. They cut the barb wire fence and he drove right up to where I was.

Before I knew it, I was in the bed of that truck and on the way to the hospital. I remember the tetanus shot and being placed on an x ray table and Doctor Knowles probing the wound and ordering more x rays. Family and friends had arrived. I became worried looking at all those long faces. I felt better when my dad's boss came in and asked to see the wound. He lied, saying, "That's simply a flesh wound. You'll be fine, son". Shortly there after I was on my way to the operating room.

Later the doctor explained that had I not just eaten lunch the bullet might have missed me—on the other hand a half inch deeper and I might not have made it. The bullet had entered the left side of my tummy and exited about two inches to the right of my belly button. I was under sedation for three days and spent ten days in the hospital. I must have read six or seven Zane Grey novels about the old western days—with no TV—not even a radio. But after ten days, I was off and running like nothing had ever happened.

Soon thereafter things begin to change. Dino went off to Greece with his mom and his sister. Buddy ended up getting married in the tenth grade. And my family moved to California in the eleventh grade.

Our lives took us all in different places and situations. But on occasions we would meet and get to know each others' families. As we aged and retired, we came back together in Colorado Springs and kind of relived those old days. We talked with kids at the Boy Scout camp and Lake Manitou. We went back to Cripple Creek—which is now a tourist attraction. Divide has changed—that little old "Hamburgers and Chili" place is long gone.

As we became less mobile and more aged, we would frequently call each other on a Saturday morning and BS about those good old days .Well, we lost Buddy at age 82 and Dino he left us at about 86. And now it's just me—almost 90. Now if the phone rings on a Saturday morning I think, Is that Dino or Buddy? Then I quit dreaming. Life goes on.

First Choice

Dick Spence heard the faint chop, chop, chop of a distant helicopter and knew his back was broken. Wracked with pain and wondering how he had made it through the night. Dick knew help was on the way. He felt relief, guilt and disbelief. He had only wanted to impress his new wife because of her 'Ex'—that guy who had it all.

Why did June fall in love with me, Dick thought, trying to comfort himself through his pain, is one of those his most happiest life mysteries. And this once, he wanted to impress her and her kids—do something special, different—a superb gift—the Hawaiian Islands.

During the night, lying in the rocks, he had woken up after the crash. Gazing straight up, Dick had never seen so many stars in the sky. Brilliant. Sparkling.

Through the deeply carved canyon, there came the slewing of the wind, mingled with the tang of engine fuel, smoke, and the distant salt of the ocean. He could hear someone moaning. He didn't know who, only that it was a man—not June; his new wife or the girls. It was either the pilot or the guide.

Before that—he remembered the explosive loud crack, the concussive lurch, the helicopter blades striking the canyon wall—the shatter of rocks, the tumbling, the panic and screaming inside the 'copter cabin.

Before that—enjoying the pilot's angling hover so his passengers could see the one extremely rare, yellow—not pink—Ginger tree in the canyon below.

Before that—they were getting one of the best arial views of the Napali Coast on the west side of Kauai Island, including pilot's awe-inspiring tour through central Kauai's massive deep canyons—as grand as any viewed in the mainland.

Before that—he, his excited wife and two little step-daughters boarding the 'Napali-Expedition' Helicopter for the arial tour of Kauai and the Napali Coast.

Before that... Over breakfast, their other fun choices were; 'Luau' or snorkeling—and he had wanted to make this one count.

Victoria K. Begley

My House

A half-hidden 'Arc'
Lost to weeds—time
Inside, all is dead
But before the interior died
Its children fled—I fled
Now, all that stands are lichened stone walls
Windows framed in rusted iron
Roof, long ago, weathered away—my house opened wide
Received the rain
Empty rooms are filled now
With songs of a new generation
The Mayflies….
Rising in the warm evenings
Singing the glory of My House.

Taco

Taco with my last love. It was love at first sight. Taco was a rescue dog who rescued me and my dog Pettie from loneliness and boredom. We met at my friend Michelle's home, in Palm Springs. She had rescued him from the Indio Animal Shelter; where he had been too long without being adopted, possibly due to his age—approximately 10 years old. Michelle was his last chance before being euthanized. She would foster him until, hopefully, some kind soul would select him from her animal adoption website. Taco was a four pound, short-haired, light beige, doe-faced Chihuahua with ears almost as big as his little head. Due to the loss of his front teeth, his tiny pink tongue internally hung out from his tiny draw.

When I entered Michelle's home of at least 17 cats and a dog, Taco ran up to me pitifully whining for attention. I picked him up, cuddled, and petted him until it was time for Michelle and me to leave to go to dinner. He followed me to the door, whining and crying, trying to squeeze through the door as we left.

I returned a couple of days later to visit with Michelle. On seeing me, Taco ran up, whining to be picked up. Again I held and cuddled him. We were becoming attached to one another. After a while, I set him down and watched him interact with the cats. All were more than twice his size, but he held his ground. As he moved among them, they hurried out of his path, and if he wanted their space to lay on, they quickly gave it up.

I did not consider adopting Taco because I had Pettie, my paraplegic, nine pound, black and dark tan, doe-faced Chihuahua—who required much care and energy. Pettie had been injured at the doggie park. The vet had said, she had never seen a dog with this type of disc injury walk again. She advised he be euthanized. I took Pettie to my Chiropractor, who told me he had had success with disc injuries. The treatment was not successful. I kept Pettie, determined to care for him as best I could. I rationalized paraplegic people are part of society. Why not Pettie?

At this time Michelle needed hip replacement. She arranged for friend, a fellow animal rescue woman to foster Taco, while she had her surgery and recovery. Just before Michelle went to the hospital, her friend fell and broke her arm. Taco had nowhere to go. Immediately, I volunteered to foster Taco.

Taco was with me a few days when my furnace malfunctioned. I was in no hurry to get it fix as my home was a small condo with wall-to-wall carpeting and I was always cooking, baking or had soup simmering in the tiny kitchen. But Michelle became concerned. She panicked and sent a professional dog sitter friend to pick up Taco. I was devastated. Grieving. I watched Taco go.

Two days later, Michelle called. Frantic, she cried, "Come get Corky. My furnace went out. Corky's feet are getting frozen on my concrete floors." (Taco's name was Corky at that time.) Michelle had not replaced her carpeting and she had a larger and colder condo. Overwhelmed with emotion, I practically ran over to pick up Taco. Taco was mine from that day on. I signed the adoption papers immediately.

The three of us—Pettie, Taco and I—lived lovingly and happily together. Pettie and Taco loved each other. Taco seldom left Pettie's side. Pettie allowed Taco to play the alpha dog with him. We would go out for two hour walks. Pettie road in a carriage I pushed. Until I realized Taco had to jog to keep up with us, then I put him in the carriage with Pettie. They both rode side-by-side. Occasionally, I had Taco walk a little for exercise.

Pettie died peacefully June 5th, 2018. And there was only Taco and me. We both missed Pettie. Taco more so, as he stayed home alone when I had errands to run. Taco would cry when I would leave and cry when I returned home. After Pettie's death, Taco aged fast; no longer running, he walked. He lost weight. His hair thinned and he turned lighter. He whined more and more. He developed cataracts. One day, I put him in a grocery bag and took him to eat with me at a fast food. As he lay quietly at the bottom of the bag, he smelled the food and out poked his little head, sniffing at the food. There were four teen boys sitting near us. When they saw him, they laughed. One said Taco looked like a dead fish. They all giggled. One of them said, "I'm sorry, miss. He's cute." Their boyish laughter did not bother me. It did not change who he was—my little Taco. Now without Pettie to sleep beside or top of, Taco slept under my pillow. I would carry him outdoors for fresh air and set him down to walk for exercis. He wobbled, walking slowly, but did not give up. On the final day, he stopped eating. He no longer had the strength to swallow. Taco died December 1st, 2018. I buried him next to his brother, Pettie, under the aged pine tree in our rear garden. I made them a memorial with stepping stones, plants and ceramic rabbits, where I go to meditate and to remember my two little ones.

Mary Rodriguez Briggs

The Cantankerous Old Man's Paramour

drive me home
slow down
not too fast
watch the lights
red—stop
green—Go Go
help me out of the car
hold open the door
these stairs seem to get steeper all the time
wait, wait, my foot's stuck
lift it up—not too rough
hold open the door
don't let it bang my head
I'm famished
cook me dinner
it's spicy
when will you ever learn to cook?
help me bathe
wash my back
scrub my feet
you're tickling me—that's enough
put on the TV
louder, louder—I can't hear a thing
what did he say?
what nonsense

fluff my cushions
my feet are cold—there are frozen solid
I want a snack
pudding! what else do we have?
well, OK
where are my dentures?
what did you do to them?
you're always hiding them
stop shaking my arm—you'll break it!
I was not asleep
I don't wanna go to bed, not yet
I'm watching this program
quit trying the boss me around!
I rule here! why did I ever marry you?
no, not because I needed a nursemaid
because I needed you, my love
hahaha! where would I ever get such a cheap nurse?
I hope she didn't hear that
what? no love
I didn't call you
I didn't say anything

Mary Rodriguez Briggs

Voices

"Yesterday, my love, you said you erased all the graffiti on the wall. How?" I asked.

"I sprayed it off. It is a criminal act," you replied.

I answered, "It is an act of desperation. An act of hope. A cry for help. It is the reaching out for recognition, for understanding, for a place in our society. A hunger for expression. A cry for love. It is the disenfranchised war cry against fear, injustice and poverty. This simple act is their part in the struggle for survival. It is their crossing of the Delaware with Washington. It is their raising of the American Flag at Iwo Jima. It is their Remember the Alamo. In their hearts, they are saying God Bless America and God bless me, too. And America The Beautiful. And so am I. They are the outcast, the downcast, the wounded, those struggling for survival. Crying out, I'm here. I'm human, too. I, too, am human. Look at me. See me. Listen to me. Hear me. Like me. Love me. I belong. I want to belong. I desire to belong. I long to belong. I do belong.

"My love, we may erase the graffiti on the wall, but not the man. We have only cleaned the wall. Cleared his canvas for another day."

GEORGETTE BUCKLEY

After The Rain

Crisp, clean air and mind
sweet wildflowers
musky algae
greening the pond.

Drake quack-quacking
Paddling aligns
Swiftly swim
A-way

Med-i-ta-tion
Painting serenely
Har-mon-y
Bliss-s-s-s-s

Then it comes to me:
My keys are locked in the car!

GEORGETTE BUCKLEY

S. Ana

Dry, moisture-robbing winds
up your nose
stuffing your entire sinuses
Sneezing for relief

Asphalt, hot as lava
brown, smoggy sky
Late sixties
Inglewood, California

In stifling, polyester jumper
ugly, yellow and brown plaid
sweating standing still
near shady, brick, two-story
out of age, designated girls play area

Asphalt, hot as lava
melts invisible gum
stuck my sister's shoe to the ground.
Rescued by school nurse.

Georgette Buckley

d'l'r'us

'Ello Mmmm,

Vat ss 'ong vit
bing ing ing ing
d'l'r'us? Ss unmf
v ah h h...
u b 'apy 'n rchy
shp'n 'ly wy
n kd lv'n eeeee!
4'vr 8np n
aftn wtrn pnts
grn Lt tnl shh
vog,

Atr oL

@ d'l'r'us

My cryptic code is a
hybrid of 'text-ease',
mesmerizing graffiti
American slang and
maybe some Yiddish.
Spoken with a bit of
a southern twang
    think Huckleberry Finn
and/or beloved ancestral Polish
It simmers and melds into
a symphony of de-lir-i-um

Georgette Buckley

Flip-Flop

Waiting for the flip
To drop
would be a flop
Trippin'
Tick- et to no where
I dare
You to care
To assist to no—
Where
Across the pre-ci
Peace-ful
Of air
Fair
On a day so sunny
Ice cream drips
Off sticks
Sticky icky gooey
Stuck to bottom
Of my flip
flopped

My friend's mom-in-law
Passed
News on FB
We offer
Sym-path-y

Crying e-mo-gis
Though we nev-er
Knew her
Dates entered into
iPhones
as a tree branch
sn-aps
And I trip
On my flip-
Flop

Natalie Michele Champion

Alone

Wandering the city streets,

I don't miss your confining ways.

Breaking from your tethers,

I am free to

Not be society's version of the perfect wife.

A role I could never fulfill

No matter how hard I tried.

I am taking back my life.

Piece by piece,

One step...

One day at a time.

Natalie Michele Champion

Ethereal Life

Along the sunny shore on a warm, spring day,
My footprints mar the sand,
Am I really here?
Or am I a lovely apparition?
A wanton dream you dreamt last night?
Am I really here to love you?

Natalie Michele Champion

Follow the Raven

Above the ocean it flaps its wings
Where is it going?
Shall I follow it?
Or stay here along the shore,
Another sedentary rock,
Waiting to turn into hot, molten lava,
Running down the ashen,
Sleeping volcano.

Natalie Michele Champion

Lost

Darkness
Driving
Opaque edges
No one to ask directions
There I see
An old, gnarled homeless lady
Picking up dead birds along the roadside.
How do I get home
when I don't know where I am?
How do I find my way
When I don't know where I am going?

Natalie Michele Champion

Our Bridge

The bridge that connects us,
Our love,
Our lives entwined,
Our hearts beating as one,
In rhythm with each other.

Train To Salvation
Faith is hope in things unseen.

Mild panic. The girl would not stand or sit. She refused snacks and water. I was afraid to lose her. "We take her to the hospital now." Mama took the girl into her arms.

Mama lay the girl on the hospital bed and cried. "I'm almost sorry that we came." "No, Hija, no."

In Guatemala she been saying, "Mama, if you need money, sell my clothes". She was saying it again.

The doctor asked, "Spanish only?"

"I can translate".

"So can I. I'm a man of many surprises. Do they live in a migrant shelter?"

The migrant shelter was called Assumption House. The Migra would bus in families with small children. We would offer them showers, clean clothes, and assistance to get them on their way.

The doctor asked, "Do you have other children like this? What about the adults?"

"The kids are bouncing around. The adults are going about their business".

The girl did not like the needle. Someone had donated a huge box of rosaries to the shelter. The Migrants wore the rosaries around their necks. The girl did not want to take hers off. Mr. X-Ray Tech said, "Amor, I'll give it back just as soon as I'm finished."

"Mama, I'm cold."

"That happens when they put in a lot of water and medicine. Find a nurse. Ask for a blanket". Mama tucked the blanket around her child. Mama was surprised to find that the blanket was already warm.

The nurse offered a choice of videos. Monster U would not have been my choice, but by the end of the video mother and child were laughing. Mama was giving the girl snacks and ice. Another video choice – Zootopia. I was hoping to see Judy Hops and Nick Fox, but the doctor came in with discharge papers.

"Are you happy that you came?"

Mama answered "Yes. We don't have anything like this in Guatemala. Here everyone treats us with respect."

"Anyone hungry?" Mama and daughter had never seen so many kinds of healthy food. "Take whatever you want." I had to choose for them. Tacos and chicken to share.

"Corn Flakes, Mama". Mama insisted that Corn Flakes were dessert. The girl was coloring.

"Red or green apples?" I asked.

"In Guatemala, we have both, but red is best."

"Are you going to be a doctor or a nurse when you grow up?"

"An artist."

"In America we have yellow apples, too". The artist was skeptical.

We waited outside as a train was going by. The girl was jumping up and down with giggles each time a car passed. Mama asked, "Is that La Bestia?" - a mega freight train that goes from Guatemala to the US border. In English – "The Beast". Mama had seen a video of a man who had lost both legs when he slid off the top of La Bestia.

"That's an ordinary Texas freight train. There are so many trains in Texas that cowboys sing songs about them."

Excited again, the girl said, "We sing a song in church, The train to salvation."

Mother and daughter were from Chimaltenango. "The town where the indigenous people wear embroidered clothes?" Mama was surprised and happy that I had seen her town. Mother and daughter took a bus from Guatemala to the US border. Then

Mama carried her daughter through the desert along the Wall to El Paso where they surrendered to the Migra.

"They packed the women with children into a room so small that we could hardly move. It was cold. Finally, they brought us to you."

Mama came from Guatemala knowing no one. Someone from Annunciation House found a sponsor in New York. Mother and daughter left on the AmTrak. As I watched the kids in the Shelter, I thought, "One of these may be a future American Nobel Prize winner in Medicine.

Strike

My dad was a working man. After he died, I found his unions cards with receipts. "Paid in Full."

The cartoon man looked like my dad. He had a lunch box, but I saw smoke stacks. My dad worked on airplanes. The man's name was "Labor". I didn't know anyone by that name. My dad was by the apricot tree with his friends. He was doing arithmetic problems out loud and fast. Sister would give him a gold star for his notebook, maybe two. He said, "With that I could buy a gallon of milk." His friends agreed.

"I'll be late. Union meeting." Lee was resigned. She said nothing. "Mom, what's a union meeting?" "It's something that men do." After several nights of union meetings, "We're going out on strike." Lee looked worried. "Mom, what's a strike?" "It's something that men do."

After a time, Lee looked happy again. "Your dad got a job working on Ike's plane." I asked, "Who is Ike?" Lee reminded me. "You saw his picture in the Weekly Reader that Sister gave you." I recalled a smiling man with a bald head, probably someone's grandfather. Next question: "Why does Ike have an airplane?" Lee's answer: "Because he's the President." Sister hadn't explained that part. I imagined that Ike was a pilot. Why have a plane if you don't fly it? But Sister hadn't explained that part either. I'd have to ask her about it.

More good news: "Your dad got milk and sandwiches from Ike's plane." I remembered that Dick had just been talking about getting milk for us. Ike must have heard something, so he sent us milk, and sandwiches, too. Ike must have sent milk and sandwiches home to all the kids. It wouldn't be fair to leave anyone out.

Bebo had come all the way from Texas. Dick and Bebo were

on the roof with tools. When the sun went down, they switched on the new flood light. Kids got to play an extra hour.

I asked Bebo if electricians had a union. Bebo answered, "Texas is a Right to Work State". I was mystified. I saw my dad go to work every day, but I still asked, "Does my dad have a right to work?" "Sure enough, we both have a right to work, but your daddy got a union. California's not a Right to Work State." Something wasn't adding up. When I was in college, my smart-ass brother came up with the perfect answer. "Right to Work means you get to work, but they decide what to pay". I had an intuition from Bebo that grown-ups confused people by calling things what they were not. This turned out to be a valuable lesson that still holds today. Thanks, Bebo.

If I was...

If I was a shape, what shape would I be? Tall - like an Amazon tree, thin reaching high through shade to the sky and sun above - just to be me.

If I was a movement, what movement would I be? A step – one at a time, pausing here and there – to smell flowers, watch the bees, and listen for the raven -finding his high place – and for the humming bird flying to see flowers. Then stepping again, one, two three.

If I was a color, what color would I be? Flashing gold, tried by fire, shiny and bright like a Treasure Island pirate Doubloon, but also as soft as your hair streaked with golden brown in the sun splash.

DEBORAH CLIFTON

Pure Adventure

Holy measure ignites inside each child
Running and playing in this wild
Beating the pathway with a forceful gain
Overcoming walls of hurt and shame

Listen to heartbeats—sounds of the shore
Reminding us daily, it's worthy to explore
A perplexing journey arrives in the mind
Past, present, future space to find

All is textured with oracles of light
Hope and redemption in plain sight
Casting images while living the tale
Signs and wonders will truly prevail

Dawning of the season guides the way
Honor thy will for pace to stay
Engrave the values with firm salute
Open discovery is purely mute

Standing the horizon will always be
Summoned by a master in full degree
Invoking sweetness dripping from stone
Hail the rapture of glory's tone

Deborah Clifton

Pure Intention

Blending softly with inner depth
Slowly unrolling the core labyrinth
Delivering messages of faith and hope
Rendering tranquillity's ultimate scope

Beaming radiance sweet as came
Humbled honor is to gain
Sacred revelations upon the soul
Wondrous miracles making whole

The beating heart of hourglass
True intention of earthly class
Breath of life speaking free
Mastering will always be

Available to touch and to hold
Versions reaching every fold
Collective motion turns the fire
Endless possibilities transpire

Reflective pages of created history
Vastly shining the path of mystery
Encasing marbles with divine intent
Presenting gifts of heavenly scent

Deborah Clifton

Merry Endeavors

Spirit surrounds and is always near
Expanding attention away from fear
Faithfully surrendering to the divine
Comforting solace love so fine

Resting sweetly at the bliss found here
Vibrations covering all with good cheer
The innermost being now felt inside
Exposed in truth that can never hide

Within a source we enter this new frontier
Opening doors that timely appear
Centering on the highest good
Sending what needs to be understood

Bask in this presents—let it overflow
Radiance of shower, pure afterglow
Light and sorry ever so free
Into the heights of this mystery

Rejoice in the journey as you play
Gifts and talents to fulfill your day
Blending union of heart and soul
Blazing fire— cherishing the goal

Deborah Clifton

Vibrant

Unspoken words beam and register
Ripple of facts soft as a feather

Curiosity turns to face direction
Aware of cosmos eternal sensation

Grateful to observe and receive this seed
Reflection grows close this mystical deed

For hence the hour of redemption
Opening channel for heartfelt connection

Grace and beauty and now multiply
On the wings of a clear blue sky

Soaring expanding with new delights
Reaching magnificent turquoise heights

Beloved Beauty

Arise O spirit and let those see
Truth is mastered and held free
To dream creations once hidden by
The softness and wonder of moonlight sky

Ruffles unveil the mystery
And live inside the curiosity
Embellish the splendor of the gift
Presented in whole to uplift

Proclaim the divine in present moment
For the beauty and lines during comment
Boldly resting and tranquil gaze
Wondrous creation listed from haze

AARON CRAIG

The Sky Is Torn

Little Esther rose from her sleep
She jumped out of bed and onto her feet

As she did the day before and the day before that
She ran to the window to see where she was at

She knew the earth did spin and marveled why she never fell
Off in the distance, she heard the church bell

Then, on tiptoe she peered high as she dared
What's that? Could it be? Yes, the sky had a tear!

It was ever so slight and ever so small
"The sky is torn," she barely squeaked out the call

There as she stood and before she could turn
A hand reached down, it was gentle and firm

In a split second, in the blink of an eye
"The hand" fixed the tear. It fixed the sky!

Little Esther learned a lesson, from that day on
Just because you're alone, not everyone is gone.

Diana Dolphin

Imagine This

Imagine this:

You are young— say in your early twenties—you're in college living away from home for the first time in your life and you tell yourself: Hey, I've been a role player all these years lock-stepping into place. All the teachings of your very traditional grandparents, ringing in your ears. Did I mention a minister for a grandfather? And yet secretly, you've been watching episodes of Sex In The City with your friends— wide-eyed to know the existence of women like Samantha and men like Mr. Big.

Now imagine:

You think of yourself as a modern woman— the women in Sex In The City are modern right? They are true feminists— treating men like Kleenex, not letting relationships anchor them down. And you think: Wow! What have I been missing? But, smart you, you hang back. Watch your friends all tumble down that rabbit hole.

Now imagine:

Your first four years of college blow by like a blur. Your friends— bless their hearts—between their emergency abortions (how many nights did you sit by their bedsides nursing them through depression?) and the chain-popping antibiotics (what's a little STD amongst the truly enlightened?). You remain circumspect; slogging your way through government job after government job— your grandmother's voice ringing in your ear: Your reputation is everything.

In the meantime you've become cynical as well as judgmental, commitment phobic yourself; but not ready to spread the love around like your jug buddies. The men you date are baffled and bewildered when you disappear like a wanted woman the minute they hint at buying you any kind of jewelry or don't return their calls and change your number surreptitiously determined "the phone will once again be your friend", when you discover that you can just give out your pager number and blithely ignore the fifteen pages from your latest almost-long-term boyfriend.

And finally you imagine:

Yes, you didn't travel the road your friends traveled— derailing their college educations by poor choices. And yes, you put your career ahead of your relationships. But somewhere down the line, though you didn't treat men like Kleenex, you discover you were just as commitment phobic as your erstwhile liberated friends.

Seascape

It doesn't seem to matter how many times I see one; scenes of the seashore always make me sentimental. I know I am not the only one. Maybe it's the vastness of the ocean that makes us question our significance or our place on the earth. We are shown what the world could look like without us.

The seascape might represent endless possibilities, a new life on the island just across the channel or someplace over the horizon half a world away. Is there something better out there? For most of us, I suspect the sentiments are tied to more personal memories of our own seashore and seaside adventures.

In this painting the eye is first drawn to the setting sun. It is still just high enough to emit white light from its center, but also just low enough in the sky where the light is starting to turn yellow and then orange in concentric rings around the sun. Yellow light is being reflected off the water and it backlights one of the breaking waves. Beyond the waves, the ocean varies in shades of blue and emerald except where the water roils it into a white foam breaking against a rocky cliff. At the base of the cliff are rock outcroppings and tidepools where the water is calm. There are some clouds in the sky, which are turning gray, the sunlight no longer strong enough to penetrate their depths. The clouds don't appear threatening. Perhaps they are remnants of a past storm or just the beginnings of the cloud-bank covering the coastline each night. On the horizon sits Catalina Island, a gray shadow.

I am not alone looking at this scene. A couple of surfers are doing what surfers do when they're not surfing; they're surveying the water and talking about surfing. To the left it looks like there's a wave with a pretty good peak. It wouldn't be a long ride, though, so close to the rocks. This would be a nice time to be out on the water. The winds from the afternoon have died, so the shape of the waves isn't messed up by wind chop.

Better still, though, would be surfing at Huntington Pier—where the beach is long, straight, and sandy. But there's something about that place, maybe the way the pier affects the ocean bottom, resulting in a consistent break, so you can catch a lot of good rides. It's kind of crowded there, but most of the surfers pretty much know what they're doing. The conversation turns to the past, recalling the great rides we had last winter. Or the time sea lions played in the surf right next to us. Well, maybe they weren't playing, just hunting. Still they looked like they were having fun.

Off to the side there is a young couple standing arm in arm; looking at the sunset. They're honeymooning here and appear very much in love. They look comfortable with each other, talking quietly, smiling, and gently touching. It's a romantic time of day. A pensive time. Today's bustling has subsided and they're looking forward to a quiet dinner out;, then returning to their hotel for the night. They had considered going up the coast for their honeymoon but decided the drive just wouldn't be worth it. Besides, they both love this place. Now it will be even more special to them.

"C'mon, let's go!" The serenity of the scene is shattered by a child's shouts.

"No. Wait, Honey," answers his mom. "Waves are breaking too close to the tide pools. The tide is coming in, and it'll be dark soon. We'll explore the tide pools next time."

"No, it isn't. Look, no waves!"

Just then a wave crashes over the ledge and into the pools.

"Awww, we never get to ...," the little boy's whining fades as they trudge up the steps to their car.

As I watch them leave, a wave breaks behind me, and I waken with a start. For a moment I don't know where I am or the time of day. Then I recognize my room, and, of course, I'm in bed. My eyes settle on the painting on the wall, and I remember my dream.

I don't know whatever became of my surfing friend. My wife died a while back and the kids have moved away. So, here I lie. I remember the day it dawned on me that there would be no new memories made from the confines of my bed, and then the wave of sadness washed over me. All that I have is the memories already made. So, I settle in for another day of combing my past, searching for forgotten scenes.

Hey, remember the time that plane landed on the beach? And us standing there frozen with our mouths hanging open, trying to make sense of what we were seeing. And the pilot, remember him hopping down from the wing? He looked at us and just grinned and shrugged. My God, that was funny!

Constance Jameson

The Long Road Part 1

This long, long road I travel
Is ofttimes lonely and bleak.
It's a hard path and does not lead
To the peace and happiness I seek.

Along this long, long road I travel
Others do not care.
My path in life is so hard
While others' lives are easy and fair.

Walking this long, long road I travel
Hope keeps me warm
Even though it's sometimes swept away
During life's many storms.

Traversing this long, long road I travel
The cold, falling rain
Echoes my flood of falling tears,
Wishing I could forget my sorrow and pain.

During this long, long road I travel
Road signs are so unclear.
Dangers lurking up ahead
Fill my heart with fear.

Sometimes on this long, long road I travel
I come to a fork in the road,
Wondering which way I should follow,

Which way will lighten my load.

Journeying this long, long road I follow
The end is hidden from view.
Rough, winding stretches seem endless.
Easy, smooth ones seem few.

Despite this long, long road I travel
My heart can still find cheer
Just knowing He, my companion,
Is always walking near.

Constance Jameson

The Long Road Part 2

Through wisdom of my years,
I view my journeys
With anticipation, not with fears.

I trudge through cold, wet rain,
Realizing rainfall is needed
For the beauty of nature we gain.

Even though unknowns may cause harm
My friends and family are out there
To walk with me, arm-in-arm.

Instead of looking at the scary abyss,
I turn around and look
At spectacular mountains I'd miss.

Despite my fear of the dark, dark night,
Overhead are stars to guide me
Little twinkling beacons of light.

Its value I've learned to measure
Not by its little pains,
But the abundance of its pleasure.

I'm so thankful it is this long.
I'm blessed to make this journey.
Let this praise be my grateful song.

CONSTANCE JAMESON

Mirror, Mirror

Mirror, Mirror on the Wall
Who is the fairest one of all?
Well, as anyone can see,
It most certainly is not me!

These wrinkles and age spots
Oh, what a sight!
It seems they
Just multiplied overnight.

Those lotions and potions
Do absolutely no good.
How silly of me
To think they would.

They promised me skin
Smooth as a baby's behind.
Yet all they removed
Is my money, I find.

So, there'll be no more
Of my hopeful trials
Of enticing products
From cosmetics aisles.

The real solution is —
As I walk down the hall,
I just pass you by,
Mirror, Mirror on the Wall!

Constance Jameson

Pen

I am Pen.
It is said that I am mightier than the sword.
Oh, so true!

Consider this — I, along with my pal, Paper — am powerful,
affecting — even controlling — individuals, families,
   communities, countries.

I can be classy, presented as gift,
or plain, like from a hotel or dollar store.
My ancestors, the Fountain Pen, the Quill, were just as powerful
   as I.

   Let's look at the power I can wield — just forming letters into words, words into sentences, sentences into paragraphs, which evolve into documents, stories, and books. Affecting people, over and over again, in both positive and negative ways.

Love letters, "Dear John" letters, marriage licenses, divorce decrees
Birth certificates, death notices
Diplomas, failure notices
Acceptance notices, rejection notices
Home mortgages, foreclosures
Declarations of war, peace treaties

Yes — just as with the sword,
It is important that I am handled wisely, with great care,
Knowing my might and power is held in your hands.
Knowing that, with a few strokes, I can change lives
Lives of others — and perhaps even you.

CONSTANCE JAMESON

Dream's Lament

I am Dream Unfulfilled
Left behind for lack of time, energy, resources.
Left behind because someone scoffed, thought me too lofty,
too foolish.

Here I lie discarded
No! Not discarded — just waiting.
Waiting for you to pick me up, dust me off,
care again.

Do it. Do it now.
For I know you are not the same person you were
when you dropped me, left me, forgot me.

Wait! Forgot me? No!
You didn't really forget me.
I've been there — in your mind, your heart, your soul — waiting.

Waiting for you to try again
Try harder, try a different way.
I'm now a little seed, a nugget, a spark, just waiting,
waiting, waiting.

Perhaps now —
Now you are ready — ready to do your part.
Ready to take me, cradle me, nourish me, cherish me.

Ready to help me
So that I am not longer a Dream Unfulfilled.
No longer a Dream. No! Now — a Beautiful Reality!

Joan Jones

Surplus—The Greatest Un-wash

It's that time of the year. It's Thanksgiving or is it Christmas. Just insert 'a religious holiday of preference'. Or simply call it, 'Retail Holiday'. My bad. The same thoughts, thoughts of close families and friends or even frenemies. Gosh if only we can put a few dollars in an envelope. But we can't. There's a way of doing things and they all expect a 'be happy don't worry' attitude. Well good luck with that. Somebody, please get the baseball bat. Ok, no violence, cheers all around, but go easy on the sauce.

Let's get out there and retail. In short, get them what they want, not what they need, after all, birthdays and other events will be happening throughout the year.

Our society is burdened with surplus food, clothes, cars—you name it, it's available if you're willing to pay for it with actual cash or credit. Pay now or pay later, but you will pay—plus interest. We have everything life has to offer, and we revel in it, brag subtly or openly about it. Let's face it, we are at the top of the food chain, predators of the have and have-nots.

With the improvements made possible by technology, the human existence remains essentially the same. We pretend to be generous and some of us are genuinely generous, however, most of the human populous tends to ignore surplus humans. There I said it. Those human beings who are all but invisible 360 days of the year. We see them as casting blight on our societal norms. They are the ultimate have-nots. These surplus beings are neither seen or heard, therefore, they're considered not relevant. Why are they relevant?

For a society which bases its morals on the Christian faith, the walk is too arduous for most people. It's amazing how many chose to forget the part of the bible which speaks about the Good Samaritan. Is Jesus represented well? Is the reason for the season, Jesus or retail coma?

All around us we hear, "It's the most wonderful time of the year." Not for the surplus people, it's just another day and another chance of going hungry, feeling cold, or not sheltered for a fleeting moment may change because the non-surplus feels generous. But for the surplus, there's no end to a miserable existence in sight for them, except death.

For every action, there's an equal reaction. Every problem has a solution if only the non-surplus would find the will to find the solution to homelessness. Exponential growth of the surplus could engulf the non-surplus eventually.

Joan Jones

Unknown

I'm afraid, but not of fear
It's cold, getting colder, can't control it
I'm afraid it's wetter, no shelter

Basket overflowing
Not with food,
Basket overflowing,
Only with 'maybe'

Maybe I can use it tomorrow
I'm afraid, but I have hope
I think there's a tomorrow for me

I have now, always now
I'm human, just surplus..

Joan Jones

You Don't Matter

    Second nation laws were created and adjusted for 'them' to keep the advantage. Such privilege. What if third or fourth nations created their own laws disregarding or discarding 2nd nations laws? What if 3rd or 4th nations decided to counter 2nd nations laws with the logical conclusion of f... me, then I f... you, dust to dust, ashes to ashes?

    2nd nation belief system is one of self- importance and strength, they see kindness and integrity as weakness and therefore show no respect. So, come at 'them' on their own terms. Do not negotiate, do not take prisoners, and never apologize. Their philosophy remains leave them dead, their laws will set them free. After all who made those .... Laws.

Second nation laws
Created and adjusted
Keep the advantage
Such privilege, such self-importance

Kindness or integrity represents weakness
No respect necessary
No accountability
Predetermine laws frees 2nd nation

When third or fourth nations
Created and adjusted laws
Within the same system
War was inevitable
Dust to dust, ashes to ashes

New philosophy

No negotiations,
No prisoners
No apology
Flip the switch

If Third or fourth nations discarded
2nd nation laws

Joan Jones
Inlandia Goeske Poetry In Motion
December 29, 2019

JOAN JONES

Stop Hitching Your Wagon

Step to the side
Can he move forward without me
No movement
He's not moving
What's he waiting for

Re-hitch, no I think not
Let him move without me
I dare I dare
No movement forward
Wheels not turning
He's not moving

Go west young woman
Go west young woman

JOAN JONES

Still Here

Every day I say I see the sun
Thank You, still here

Yesterday the wind erupted, howl into dust
Thank You, still here

Yesteryear the waters flowed, mud flowed
Thank You, still here

Birds singing, cats meowing, dogs barking
Thank You, still here

Today I say, I see the day, I feel my way
Thank You, still here.

Florence Lucero

In Memory Of My Late Brother Eric

As a child, you knew no wrong
As a child, you learned to be strong
As a youth, you tended to stray
As a youth, you went your own way
As an adult, you thought you knew well
As an adult, you stumbled and fell
Later in life, you became ill and weak
The end of your life was so bleak
As you passed from this world to the next
I pray your final journal will be met
As I bid you adieu just know that I'll always
Love and miss you

FLORENCE LUCERO

Turning Point

At the crossroads I stand
My heart in hand
The future that seemed far away,
Is now here to stay
I will keep the lessons
Of a lifetime near
Friends, teachers, parents
I hold dear
Decisions I make will
Give me peace
Every one I make, I pray will be
Made to hold you all near

Phyllis Maynard

Fun Friday

What do you do with a star of pot when it's there in front of you and it practically jumped up off the walk-way to nestle itself right there in your hand?

Do we replace it where a someone—probably a student—obviously dropped it?

Do we drop it off at the University of California, Riverside (UCR) police station?

Do we throw it away?

Smoke it? No. Of course not. We don't smoke pot!

Doug, my late husband, and I were on our nocturnal roving through UCR when the little baggie of marijuana made a sudden appearance.

It was kind of exciting. In the 1970s, marijuana was a big no-no. Of course everyone has been educated about its evil effects. But, we'd also heard of the "fun" side of pot. Doug and I were curious; what could be done with this little baggie of booty. We talked of the possibilities involving "using"—putting the pot "to use".

Here was something of worth—obviously lost to its previous holder. We couldn't advertise or its owner, could we?

Doug and I continued on our walk, contemplating the future for this newly discovered contraband. We decided we'd need to contact an "expert" in the area. Not a "pot-head" but someone well-versed in the dangers and pleasures of pot.

Of course! Danny! Our seventeen year old son would be more familiar with what this baggie was all about. I never suspected or expected our kids to be 'friendly' with marijuana, but several months earlier, I'd notice Danny smelling a little "gamy". When I laundered his flannel shirts, they reeked of skunk. Well, Doug and I found out—from his informant younger brother—it was the scent of pot.

Of course, according to Danny, it was his friend doing the pot experimentation—not him. His shirts just picked up the scent.

Now, according to our seventeen year old—who claimed to only have a vague knowledge of pot—the marijuana Doug and I found was the "good stuff".

My husband and I decided, since we were in possession of "good stuff", we should do something with it to create a memory—something enjoyable to remember. We should bake brownies laced with pot and take them to the office where I work.

Now I work in a corporate office with a super conservative, old (1908) food distributor. I was in my 14th year working for A. M. Lewis, Inc. and would rather cut my throat than jeopardize my job.

But, Doug convinced me we could pull it off.

We could do this clandestine thing that would be remembered by many as the best "Fun Friday" ever.

It it was customary for the entire office to bring all kinds of goodies for "Fun Friday"— finger food, cookies, chips, fruits, nuts, etc.— when we'd all enjoy the offerings and each other's company between noon and 1:00 p.m.

The office was open at 8:00 a.m., so at 7:00 a.m., Doug dropped me off at the back entrance of the office building. With the stealth of a cat burglar, I entered the office and deposited my "offering" on the lunch table designated for the lunch goodies. The "special" brownies were on a paper plate covered with foil wrap—so the mystery was to everyone, Who brought those delicious brownies?

I dashed back downstairs to Doug waiting with the motor still running. We continued on down to University Avenue to have breakfast, then returned back to the office at 8:00 a.m. where I merrily bid everyone "good morning". Oh, it was exciting! I felt like it was going to be a fun day.

About 2:00 p.m., most of the office staff was still lingering around the lunch area—lots of laughing and camaraderie. My boss—a very proper, staid gentleman always wore a suit, white shirt, tie (the works)—suddenly took off his suit jacket (a first), loosened his tie, and announced "God. It's hot in here."

It wasn't long until all the prim, proper bosses were in shirt-sleeves—sans ties and coats.

Needless to say, not much work that done that Friday. But, there were lots of giggling and munching. It was a Friday to be remembered. It was talked about for a long time. One of the secretary said it was a "magical time of togetherness—when everything seemed just so right".

Yeah, sure. It was a magical "high".

Doug would call me every half hour asking, "What's going on now?"

Epilogue

Some years later, it was November. Time to vote. I walked to the address where I was to vote and there he was—my boss from A. M. Lewis. He was a precinct captain of the voting area

We were happy to see each other after all these years. A. M. Lewis had long since closed. He was retired. So as I. Doug, my husband, no longer my partner in crime.

So I told him the "big secret"— how Doug and I drugged the entire office force (him included) on "Fun Friday".

I never saw him laugh as hard as that day in all the years I worked with him.

Tempest

We were sucked up in the tempest. Horrified at the unexpected assault on our lives. Fighting. Fighting for recovery. Fighting for reality. Will this nightmare ever end?

The tempest spun us around—making every sound bring pain and fear into our hearts.

For 32 days, we were swirled and swept into the dark, slashing waters of uncertainty. Half drowning. Half alive. Screaming for help. Help for us both.

Don't take him!

Take me too!

Don't take us at all!

When will this raging maelstrom ever end?

One morning appearing calm, just to be followed by another life-threatening crisis.

The thunder was deafening. Ominous.

No, not thunder, but a voice coming through loud and clear.

Was it Zeus?

Was it Thor?

Or the all-seeing eye of the Almighty?

"I'll take him.

And to show you I've got no pity to give, I'll toss you about. But I'll let you live."

When the 32 stormy days ended—with shocked disbelief of the terrible ruin and rubble of my life—a gentle, quiet rain began.

The voice came again. This time not thunder, but a soft breeze.

"No more storms. You've weathered the worst. But from now 'til you close your eyes, only sweet droplets of memory will be your journey through life."

PHYLLIS MAYNARD

Celena's Mom

Perhaps has been told
Has the patience of Job
While raising a kid like Celena

Who's friends and smart
With a mind that is sharp
While challenging life's s great arena

She was raised to be strong
And fearless along
With courage to stretch beyond reach

She's a good coach and guide
(Now, with kudos aside)
As a teach, we think you're a peach!

Vicki Urrunaga

The Watcher

There upon the barren bleachers
Drenched in droplets, all alone,
Sat the ever-hopeful Watcher
Waiting for that throw to home.

Should we tell him, dare we whisper—
In a friendly sort of way?
Shall we tell him extra gently,
"Hey Mister, there will be no game today"?

VICKI URRUNAGA

Wobzec's State

Helenix X245
Roluxia Anabogga B.D.R.

Gruudel momi gogo Inuber,

Evtru vel ete dat nini gogo Wobzec—e mega dip estimate!
Oni vel migplypah ete, izo oni vel mufti luldzah noga solas.
Penlunoo oni veslo pu ooshi plugarints suca au erge solas pu ninis ergre gogos.
Woosemo Zu soopi oni ed veshina mux exiblix au ne-sola.
Zu soopi lu sooni palla muti emital.

Synetachy, momi og,
Listrol (tuti gogo)

Marlene Mossestad

The Dream

2:00 p.m. March 12, 2001, a young, unmarried woman eighteen years of age received her test results from her doctor. She indeed was pregnant. This unwelcome revelation was certainly not what she had wanted to hear on her birthday. The rest of the day was a blur. Her thoughts went rolling around in a kaleidoscope of emotions: bewilderment, anxiety, fear, guilty, anger...

That night, she was exhausted—having spent all day trying to process the discomfiting news. She went to bed, and, after some time, fell into a deep slumber. As morning approached, she had a dream. She was in a church and beside her was a nun.

After waking, she reflected on her dream. During the rest of the day, she pondered obsessively over her dilemma. By the end of the day, she knew what she was going to do. She was keeping her baby.

November 3, 2019, she was making preparations for her dear daughter's eighteenth birthday which would be celebrated the following day. Glancing at the living room wall, she gazed warmly at the picture she painted many years ago. It as about a dream that had helped her make a decision for which she was forever grateful.

MARLENE MOSSESTAD

Scifaiku

hell-bent asteroid
barreling towards the earth
consequence unknown

Geri Olayan

Last

Lasting memories
Last year we had a family vacation
This last year was tough
The last movie was great
Our last date we had sushi
You lasted a long time
Our last dance was sweet
Our last week was special
I knew it was our last day together
Your last night we sang
I last kissed you on your cheek
Last night you slipped away
You made a lasting impression
Now, at last, you rest

Phyllis Ahpuck Reis

The Spirit Of The Law

One of my many nights of working SunnyMead and Edgemont during the summer of 1983, I was on patrol with a male ride-a-long. A ride-a-long is a civilian who requests to ride-a-long with the Riverside County Sheriff's Department. The individual must have a background check for felonies and warrant checks. We don't want "cop killers" riding with our deputies.

My ride-a-long and I are driving down Cottonwood by the old fire station and ahead of my unit I saw a pair of headlights coming towards us—head on. I maneuvered my unit out of the way of the wrong-way driver. I made a u-turn in the middle of Cottonwood and pulled the driver over. I slowly approached the errant driver to the driver's side of the vehicle. I asked him why he was driving on the wrong side of the road. He could have run into my unit. Then, the smell of alcohol from his breath and his person hit my nostrils.

I had him out of his car and tried to see if I could have him perform a Field Sobriety Test (FST). When I let go of him, he almost fell to the ground. I caught him and, with the help of my ride-a-long, we got the errant driver against my unit, so I could search the driver for weapons or contrabands.

While I was searching this man, he started telling me that he has already been in trouble with prior DUI's (driving under the influence offenses). He said he was in the Air Force, stationed here at March Air Force base, Sunnymead, California. He was a Colonel.

He explained that if he gets any more DUIs, his career in the Air Force would be over.

I am a baby Boomer—raised around World War I, World War II, Korea and Vietnam veterans. Though all law enforcement officers are trained to think on their feet and make quick decisions, I thought a long time about this decision. Should I take this man to jail and let the courts handle this? The man didn't beg or talk about his wife or kids. I told my ride-a-long to follow in the errant owner's car to the inebriated man's home. The man directed me to his house and my ride-a-long drove the man's car onto the driveway the man's house.

I walked him to the front door of his house. His wife was upset with her husband as I turned him around so I could remove his handcuffs. I told the wife, 'If he if he got out and got back behind the wheel of his car and he kills someone, I'm in the doghouse. I would be just as guilty as your husband is we're killing other people on the road.'

She had her mouth wide open and instantly understood what I was talking about.

I told her, 'I don't care how you sober him up or just put him to bed. Hide the keys and anymore spares you may have.'

I later told my ride-a-long that the decision I made to drive the man home instead of to jail was not one of my best moves, but something inside of me said, 'Phyllis, the "Spirit of the Law" would be for the next time.'

Phyllis Ahpuck Reis

The Letter Of The Law

In the year of 1984, I got one of numerous calls from our Riverside County Sheriff's Department Dispatch Center that a lady in Woodcrest says an unknown woman took her dog from their front yard.

I drove to the house then made contact with the lady who called the sheriff's office. She told me she had an unknown woman wanting to pet her dog whenever the dog owner is outside with the dog. She said she told this unknown woman to stop bothering her and the leave her and her dog alone and stay away.

The woman gave me a description of this woman and I got into my unit and drove around the area to see if I could find the woman walking with a dog fitting the description of the pet owners dog.

I saw a woman fitting the description carrying the dog. I park next to the walking pair. I stopped her and started asking her who she is and asked her for identification. While talking to her, I smelled the alcohol coming from her breath and her person.

I told her that I had a complaint that the true owner the dog wanted the dog back. If the dog was returned, to the rightful owner, the owner would not pressed charges against her. I searched the woman and put her in the back of the unit.

When I returned, to the dog's owner's home, she met me in the front yard of her driveway and squealed with happiness, when she saw her dog in the passenger seat of my unit. I gave her the dog and asked the dog owner if she was sure she did not want to swear out a complaint against the woman who took her dog. The pet owner said, 'no'.

I told my dog thief to give me directions to her own house so I could drive her home. Instead of arresting her for public intoxication and locking her in jail, I drove her home. Before I left her behind, I gave her a Field Sobriety Test.

I told her I was giving her her freedom but she had to stay away from the lady's house with the dog.

I thought she would be alright. She had a roommate. The woman has a drinking problem and tends to walk around Woodcrest under the influence. I made it my mission to drive around the area she lives to make sure she's OK. When I wasn't too busy answering calls for burglaries, assaults, family disturbances, peeping Tom's, and you name it—I'm out there trying to fight crime.

I saw her sitting on a curb on Van Buren Boulevard—a busy street that runs through Woodcrest. She saw my unit attempted to run. I caught her.

She was so drunk, she could not stand. I took her into custody and arrested her for public intoxication. She begged me all the way not to put her in jail. As she was a danger to herself, I booked her for public intoxication. I wanted her to get help for her drinking. I decided to use the "Letter of the Law".

CANDACE SHIELDS

Georgia's Little Red Riding Hood

As I roll over in bed, I smell food cooking in the kitchen. The rain is steadily dripping on the roof. The rhythm is comforting and soothing. No wonder I slept so late. The steady beat of rain on the roof lulled me into a real deep sleep. You can smell the Georgia red clay because the rain has made it wet. It must have rained all night. The red clay of Georgia is dark and slippery. I can see that from my bedroom window. Moma is up early cooking, but the smell is not breakfast food. I would have loved to have bacon and eggs with some blueberry pancakes on the side, but that is not what I am smelling. What I am smelling more like lunch or dinner. It can't possibly be that late. Moma would never let me sleep past lunch time. Life on a Georgia farm was run on a schedule and the schedule very seldom changed. Something is going on for the schedule to change so drastically. So I guess I better get up and see what's going on. I don't dare go into the kitchen before I have washed up and I am fully dressed. Moma set the rules for the house and no matter what was going on we couldn't bypass those rules. She ruled with an iron hand and she didn't forget once you committed an infraction. And one of those rules was to be fully dressed before we sat at the table to eat. Thank God I took the time to re-braid my hair last night and tied it up before I went to bed. That's one thing I won't have to worry about. I just needed to wash up and get dressed. As I put oil on my dark brown skin, it begins to glisten and feels so much better. I always found it amazing that Moma's skin is a light carmel color and Daddy's skin is a dark brown color like me. It just seems that I would have been born a cinnamon color, like my brothers. However, nature had a totally different idea. It appears at this time that I didn't get any of Moma's features. She has beautiful black hair and gorgeous hazel eyes. But I guess I get my looks from Grandma, who has stubborn hair and skin the color of Expresso. So where did Moma get her carmel color and beautiful hair? They say she got them from Grandpa Henry, but I don't' know cause I never met my grandfather. He died when I was too young to remember him.

After I made my bed, washed up and dressed I went into the kitchen to see where everyone else was and why Moma wasn't cooking breakfast.

"Good morning, Moma," I said to Moma as I turned the corner to the kitchen. Moma turned with a loaf of hot bread, right out of the oven in her hands and said, "Well, it's about time you were up and dressed." "Where's everybody else," I asked. "Your father and brothers are already gone into the field." "Since I needed you to run an errand for me this morning when I finished cooking, I decided to let you sleep in."

As I was wondering what errand Moma could possibly want me to run for her today, I sat down and started munching on a biscuit I found covered on a plate in the center of the table. I knew not to ask her outright, but to just sit down and wait. Moma would tell me in her own good time and it would be better for me to just wait.

"Red Riding Hood, your grandma is sick and I been fixing her some food for you to take to her this afternoon. So get your cape as soon as you are finished eating on that biscuit, put on your rain boots, and I will pack up the food that I have been cooking for her this morning for you to take to her."

I started to say something and thought better of it. My mother did not look like she was in the mood to argue, so I just sat there munching on the biscuit. I reached over to get some butter to put on the biscuit, while I started thinking, why did it always have to be me. It seemed that one of my three brothers could have run this errand much faster than I could have. After all Pa would let one of them drive the truck, but I knew not to question my mother in her present mood. Her mother lived a crossed the forest from us and even though it was in walking distance Moma didn't always have the time to go to her mother's house. Keeping house on a farm was hard work. Moma and Daddy worked from sun up til, sun down and even then everything didn't get done. Grandma understood cause she had been a farm wife herself before Grandpa died. After that Grandma seemed to have lost her heart for farming and just kept a small garden outside her kitchen door.

It troubled Moma that her mother was getting up in age and couldn't always do for herself, so it was up to us kids to help see about Grandma. It wasn't that I didn't love my grandmother. She was the best grandmother anyone could have. When I was over her house, I got away with a lot of things I could never get away with at home. Moma could be hard, but Grandma, was well Grandma.

Grandma's name was Ellen. She was a large woman with beautiful dark brown skin, of which she was so proud. She was the color of expresso. She always took care of her skin and she loved her colors. Grandma Ellen knew what colors went well with her expresso skin and she dressed to kill when she would go to church on Sundays. When I was younger Grandma would sit me on her ample lap and rock me in her huge rocking chair that was in her living room next to the fireplace. Those where the best memories I had of my times with Grandma. While I was munching on the last of the biscuit, I began to think about Grandma's biscuits. Moma's biscuit were great, but Grandma's biscuits were heavenly. They would melt in your mouth.

Enough remembering, I had better get going I had a ways to go and time was getting away from me. "Moma, when you want me to leave?" "Red Riding Hood, I am packing the basket now. Go get your red cape that I made you for school. Put it on, it should keep you warm and dry while you go through the forest. Now child when you get to the forest, don't take no shortcuts. I know you. STAY ON THE PATH. Don't talk to other people, especially that scoundrel Wolfie that wonders around in the forest. He is no good and he always got something to say to little girls. Especially one as pretty as you."

WoW! I thought, Moma must be feeling pretty good, cause

she don't hand out compliments every day. I was so caught up that she called me pretty that I didn't think anything about what she said about staying on the path or Wolfie. "Okay, Moma" I said, as I put on my red cape, slid into my red rain boots and put a tea towel over the food in the basket. "I better get going or I won't be able to be home for dinner."

Moma said "If I know your grandmother, she gonna keep you there all night. So I really ain't expecting you back till tomorrow morning. I packed enough food for you and your grandmother. I expect your grandmother is lonely, since she ain't feeling too good and can't get out like she's used to. So enjoy your time with your grandmother. But don't worry her none. Do any chores she ask you to do and don't tucker her out with your nonsense. You understand?"

"You must be really worried about Grandma if you willing for me to stay the night." I said as I waved at my mother and headed toward the forest. I could see my father and four brothers in the field, but I knew it didn't make sense to holler at them. They were too far away to hear me. Wait till they came home for dinner this evening and find out I was going to stay the night at Grandma's. My brothers would be mad because as the only girl in the family and the baby, I always was the one to spend the night at Grandma's since I was old enough to go to Grandma's house by myself.

It wasn't raining as hard as it was when I first got up this morning. In fact it was barely drizzling, but I kept the hood of my cape up as I started toward the forest. I didn't have my mother's hair and I didn't want it to get wet and draw up so I kept it covered. Red Georgia clay turns slippery when it's wet, so I had to pay attention to where I was stepping so I didn't slip and fall. Even though I had on my red rain boots to match my red cape, I still needed to be careful. It wouldn't due for me to slip and fall with Grandma's food. Carrying the basket full of goodies wasn't easy either. It was heavy and it smelled so good. A couple times since I started out I was tempted to tear off a piece of bread to munch on or may be take out a piece of fried chicken. It was the smell that was driving me crazy. Moma had fixed Grandma one of her favorite meals. I could tell from the smell that there was fresh bread, fried chicken, collard greens, candied sweet potatoes and sweet tea in the basket. No meal was ever served in Moma's house without sweet tea.

As I trudged through the slippery red clay, I began to think about how much fun I could possibly have with Grandma Ellen. She was getting older, but she loved to tell the stories about when she was younger and how she and grandpa had raised their family right there on the same land that her family had owned for years. That was so important to Grandma cause not everyone owned their land. Many were sharecroppers and barely scrapped out a living off the land. I had to laugh to myself, I was starting to talk like Grandma. At last I came to the edge of the forest. I was already tired from lugging that basket of food. I still had to go all the way across the forest to get to Grandma's house. Now there was a shortcut, but it wasn't really safe and I wasn't sure about taking it. Once you entered into the forest, the trees had grown together overhead and blocked out most of the light, which caused the forest to be dark. And today of all days it was going to be damp. As I was standing at the edge of the forest, I heard someone call my name. "Red Riding Hood, where you going, girl?" I turned to see who had called my name and sure enough it was Wolfie. He was about six foot tall, dark brown skin with his hair braided straight back. He was doing what he was known for doing. He was flipping a coin up and down as he leaned against a hugh white oak tree. He was dressed in a zoot suit. Who in the world wore a suit in the country on the weekday, unless they was going to a funeral except Wolfie. I didn't want him to see me laughing cause he was easily offended when he thought us kids were laughing at him. So I straightened up my face and said, "Mr. Wolfie, you scared me for a minute. I am on my way to my Grandma's house on the other side of the forest."

He answered "Red Riding Hood, why don't you take the short cut? It goes right by my house and it won't take you near as long.

I'll walk with you so you won't have any reason to be scared. I'll even carry the basket for you. We can even stop by my house, have some dessert, and rest for a minute. And you won't be late for your Grandma Ellen's. No one has to know that you stopped by my house. How does that sound to you?" As Wolfie leered at me. The looked that Wolfie gave me shook me to my very being. There had been stories about him that were whispered on the school yard about young girls that disappeared after being seen with Wolfie never to be seen or heard of again.

At first the thought of going through the forest by the short cut sounded so appealing. I didn't want to walk through the forest to get to Grandma's, but I also wanted to be able to be back home tomorrow in one piece. So I let Wolfie think that I was considering taking the short cut, but in my heart of hearts I knew I would never trust Wolfie to help me along the short cut, but I did not want to offend him. "Mr. Wolfie, as much as I would love to walk with you on the short cut, the one thing I have learned from my moma is to obey what she tells me, even when she's not around to see me. It just works out better in the end." Then I put on my most charming smile and looked straight into Wolfie's eyes. "It would be an honor to walk with you on the short cut, especially with you dressed so very nicely in your yellow zoot suit with those beautiful brown stripes. It just complements your dark brown skin, but I must be obedient to what my mother told me." Being young and naïve, it never dawned on me that by putting on my most charming smile and looking straight into Wolfie's eyes, he would think I was flirting with him. This big toothy smile crossed Wolfie's face as he tried to convince me that there was safety in numbers and how he was able to keep anything from happening to me. He even reached out to dtrokre my cheek but I managed to duck just in time. "Mr. Wolfie everything you just said souns good, but you know how people are always watching for something to talk about. I can just imagine someone seeing me going off with you and telling my mother and my mother sending my father and brothers to get me." The mention of my father and brothers didn't set too well with Wolfie and he backed off and said "I"ll just walk a piece with you and when we get to the short cut, I'll go my own way. That way I know you will be okay walking to your grandma's house. Wolfie sounded sincere and he almost had me fooled, but just when I felt myself giving in to the sound of his voice, my mother's face and voice came into my head telling me to stay on the path. And I knew I had better stop talking to Wolfie and get on my way. So I picked up my basket off the tree stump where I set it and started down the path. Wolfie started walking with me, but it just didn't feel right. In fact I was scare so I told Wolfie I had lost too much time talking to him and needed to hurry up. He was wasn't pleased but he went on his separate way. After about ten minutes of speed walking I slowed down and enjoyed my walk to grandma's house. I passed some sharecroppers working their field at the edge of the forest and it was good to know there was someone else in the forest besides me. When I got to the edge of grandma's property, I could see smoke coming out the chimney so I knew grandma was home. I hurried along a little faster cause I had worked up an appetite and could hardly wait to eat. I pushed the door with my hand and it opened, but I couldn't see anyone. "Grandma Ellen, where are you? It's Little Re Riding Hood and have I got a surprise for you." I hollered out as I sat the basket on the kitchen table. I could hear noise coming from the bedroom, but Grandma Ellen didn't answer. So I went to the door of the room and called out again, "Grandma Ellen, are you alright?" This time a strange sounding voice answered. "Is that you Little Red Riding Hood? Child, come on in and see your grandma." I walked to the edge of the bed but it just didn't look like Grandma Ellen, for one thing the person laying in the be was a lot smaller than grandma and had on a wig in bed. I had never seen grandma with a wig on in bed. The person laying in the bed had the covers pulled up so that I couldn't see her face and the voice sounded weak and thin. "Come over and sit on the side of the bed," the person laying in the bed said very softly. Now I was really worried. Grandma Ellen never allowed anyone to sit on her bed for any reason. I drew close to the bed and said "Grandma, you don't sound like yourself." Grandma Ellen said, "It's only because I am not feeling well, girl. Why don't you come closer so that I don't have to talk so loud?" As I was uncomfortable, I only moved forward a little bit. "Grandma Ellen, you don't look like yourself. Your color is off and you look so small in that bed." "Red Riding Hood, didn't your mother send you to visit me because she was worried about me being sick? Then why are you surprised that my color is off and that I have lost weight. You are making much out of nothing. Come on over here and sit down." Now I was really scared. Whoever that person was in my grandmother's bed, it definitely was not my grandmother. "Grandma Ellen, I am not going to sit on your bed, because you don't allow me to sit on the bed." I answered. "Girl, I know you are not disobeying me when I told you to come and sit on the side of the bed." You could tell the person in the bed was getting angry, so I pushed a little harder. "Not only am I not going to sit on the side of the bed, I am going to take my basket and go back home." This really made the person in the bed mad. The women in the bed pushed the covers back to reveal a yellow and brown zoot suit. It was Wolfie. I took off running and screaming. It took him a minute to get out of the bed. The house wasn't that big so I made it to the door and outside before Wolfie got close to me. I kept screaming while I was running. I remembered the sharecroppers at the edge of the forest and headed that way. I never looked behind me so I didn't know if Wolfie had followed me or not. Not too far from my grandmother's house I ran into the arms of one of the sharecroppers and told him Wolfie was after me. He ran to my grandmother's house and found Wolfie lying on the floor where he had tripped and knocked himself out on the edge of grandma's bed. The sharecropper picked up Wolfie and threw him out of Grandma Ellen's house and told him to never come near me or Grandma Ellen again. Then we went through Grandma Ellen's house to find her. As we were calling her name, we could hear muffled cries. The sharecropper opened the closet door in the front room and there was my grandmother gagged and tied up. We freed grandmother and got her into her rocking chair near the fireplace. I was so glad Grandma Ellen was okay that I wrapped my arms round her ample body as much as I could and began to cry. "Now Red Riding Hood stop crying! I am okay. I am okay! I am so glad you and this young man came back looking for me. When I answered the door Wolfie pushed his way in here and knocked me to the floor, tied me up, gagged me and locked me in the closet. I am so glad you found me." The young sharecropper left to go find Wolfie and take him to the authorities. I got Grandma Ellen to sit down at the kitchen table and I fixed us both a plate from the basket Momma sent for us to eat. Somehow food always makes a situation better. As I fixed our plates I began to give thanks that the young sharecropper had come to our aid and helped us when we really needed it. While I sat across the table from Grandma Ellen, I remembered that we never asked the young sharecropper his name. I wasn't worried though. On my way home tomorrow morning, I would stop by his field and thank him properly. Also I will ask him his name. Wait til I get home and tell them about what happened today, they will never believe this story.

Mountains

I love looking out of my kitchen windows at the mountains.

When the weather is clear I can see all the crevices.

I find my fascination with the mountains to be an oxymoron

Because I am afraid of heights, I seldom go anywhere near them

Yet the mountains symbolize stability and unchangeableness.

Every morning when I open my blinds, I am reassured.

Even after the fires the mountains basically look the same way they did the day before.

The mountains are part of my daily routine.

They aid in my meditations when I am struggling with life's difficulties,

When I look at the steadfastness of mountains

Words

These days, we've got people obsessed with words. Labels. One notes. Soundbites. Such as sexist, racist, fascist, socialist, snowflake.

Words are words. They are fine by themselves. It's our sentiments, our feelings associated with these words that cause them to conform to something we think we may know.

Words are taught to us to awaken what we try to bury. Or that we may have not seen before. We cannot understand until we see from our own hearts. Else that word stands as it is, a word that represents a thing. A something. A thing that may or may not be hurtful. Any power it may contain is only because we have felt it.

They aren't really saying that you should conform to what is deemed acceptable in society (most of the time in my experience, at least). They're a wish for children in the world to open themselves to the heart of the matter. That the soul we have can take many forms. And their end goal is love. A love felt, intangible, understood as that we must all share. We are built to have it, to want it, to see it.

But if words are said without sentiment, without a story, they close the heart. The willingness to learn, the willingness to accept, the joy of learning how to be wrong and better ourselves, our fellow man, or anything else for that matter. It dooms us to stagnation and may cause the love within us to fester. If those thoughts are left alone for too long, the words crumple. Because love does that when it's not shared. When it's not treasured.

It's like the moment you learn that Oklahoma originated from Indians for the first time. Though they were driven away from their homes and many were ill, cold, and cheated from everything they had ever known in a swindle or forced extraction, they still wanted a land to call their own. To say that they owned it and were attached to it, regardless of how "the invaders" had stolen and sneered at their existence.

Yes, the name was designated by the American invaders, and they were using it as a quarantine. Yes, it is a reality that many people in Oklahoma claim that their way of living with deep-fried foods and heart-clogging drinks is the all-American way, as if that has always been the way of the land that they have lived in and it was always in their name.

At one point, at one small precious point, the Indians wanted to accept this mandated segment of land as their own, one that was to mark them and the land as their own. One that respected their ancestors and brings to mind the times that were, not the time of enforcement. It was a land that was for them. Together we stand. We are here. A land that can be for us. Built on a lie, built on a broken promise, still, the Indians believed.

Least I think they did because I'm human. We all want a home.

In Japan, it's a cultural norm for people's names to be composed in kanji. Names that can hold multiple meanings. It was a cultural norm to adopt a character of a family member that was your senior, so that they could live on in their children and their children's children. While I'm not completely familiar with the culture and language, I'm aware that this is a trait from China. And China could have originated or reworked this tradition from India. And there are dozens of other indigenous people who do the same. All to infinity, we want that name to reflect the love that has (or been).

How many words do we think to know but end up being so alien to us?

I remember the first time I felt this way.

It was kindergarten. We were learning the colors of the rainbow and the letters of the alphabet. That was the class lesson that day, and it was with a boy I'll call Spencer.

Me and Spencer were bestest, bestest, bestest friends. We liked swinging on the jungle gym bars and swings. We made sand castles and climbed trees. We played tag and started races with the other boys. I don't think we got into too much trouble, but I do remember a lot of scraped knees. I told him I liked cats, and he got me a cute white kitty doll for my birthday. I still have it.

We liked to hold hands now and then because it was what bestest, bestest, bestest friends do. Not once did I ever question that.

One day, we'd come in from noon recess and we were sitting at our assigned seats. I had been sweaty running around in the sun and Spencer had sat next to me, as all bestest, bestest, bestest friends do.

Our seats were those tiny square desks that clumped kids together into a rectangle of five or six. I was shuffling through my desk bunk for construction paper, scissors, pencils, and crayons for scribble time. My favorite part of class.

As I was getting the crayons out and Spencer had clicked his pencil box open with those snip-snap hooks that I envied, one of the girls at our rectangle leaned as far as she could to look at Spencer like he had done a very bad thing.

I thought she was pretty-looking with her blond pigtails and blue eyes, so I looked away from her. Couldn't help it. Always shy with people who I think are pretty, and that is true even now. Maybe I was trying to remember if I had all of my colored crayons that day for the rainbow. Red, blue, orange, green...

I don't remember who said what or what sparked it, but the girl had slapped her tiny hands on table like the angry prosecutors did on TV. I looked up. It's hard not to when that happens. You want to keep going with the rhythm.

Then the girl said words that I have never forgotten to this day: "Don't hang out with her anymore. She isn't white, she's yellow!"

Yellow? That's not what the teacher taught us. I was convinced that she was talking about the color that I was missing. But when I saw her pointing at my skin, I thought she was confused

177

by the color of my suntanned forearm. My grandma always said I had such pretty white skin. Oh, look at her tiny white hands! Was the girl sunblind? All that running in the sun must have confused her.

So, I flipped over my arm to show the underside, pointing at the palest parts. I'm not yellow. See? Look, I'm white! Because that's what Grandma had told me that I was. Grandma had always said that, so it must be true. There was no yellow in there at all.

Yellow was the color of baby chicks. I was no baby chick.

The other kids at the table got real silent. They gave me the strangest looks. Spencer turned red. But I was convinced that this girl was not looking at the right part. She got it wrong and I was trying to correct her.

The girl curled her lip and narrowed her eyes. Maybe she would have said something else, but the teacher came back from lunch and class began. The girl didn't bring it up again.

After that, things weren't the same between me and Spencer. I'd ask him for a push on the swings, and he'd back away. Someone else can do that for you. You have friends that are girls, don't you?

When I wanted to share my newest masterpiece in the sandbox, I'd call out to him. Hey, Spencer. What about this? Can you see the cat? I sat in the dirt alone. Sand stained my shorts. My knees weren't as skinned from running around.

I'd swing on the jungle gyms and monkey bars. Hey, Spencer. Can you do this? Loop, loop around the bar with my knee. I could flip my entire upper body ten times straight without stopping. And each time I'd loop around, I'd see his blurred back walking away from me.

There was a gap there now. Right next to me. If someone tried to take it, I'd defend. It's taken! Go somewhere else! When I looped around the bars, I made sure to keep the ones next to me open, the ones at Spencer's height. Even when I saw him playing with other boys, I saved them and waved at him. These are yours. Spencer, come here!

Nothing.

I don't remember how long it took. Days, weeks, hours, minutes. Eventually I had given up on trying to convince him.

When the other boys weren't looking or nearby, every now and then after school, Spencer would chance a tiny wave in my direction before our mothers came to pick us up. It'd be one of the few times he'd meet my eyes. I would wave back, of course, always delighted.

Then one day, Spencer came up to me. I smiled, how ready I was to forgive whatever that had set us apart. Let's just play together like we always did again, I had wanted to say. Because we're bestest, bestest, bestest friends.

Spencer looked over his shoulder, maybe to see if there were other boys or if his mother was coming. He looked me in the eyes and pleaded in a tiny voice. We should be normal. Boys play with boys and girls play with girls. You have friends that are girls, don't you?

What he was talking about? We're talking now, and there's nothing wrong with that. Mommy and Daddy can talk to one another just fine. They do a lot of things together too. What makes it different between us? Does this mean he doesn't like me anymore?

I didn't think anything had gone wrong at all. A simple misunderstanding.

He turned and walked away. I think we still shared classes after that. I'd see him here and there since we went to the same school. But as far as talking to one another, that was the last time.

It's not like I was ignorant of how I was different. I was a girl who didn't like sports all that much, but I did the "boy" things like sliding in the dirt and collecting bugs. I didn't dress like a girl on most days, with my dark blue hand-me-down shorts and shirts from my older brother. I liked to draw and read, sneaking away into the school library whenever I could.

And being one of the few Japanese kids—the only one in some years—in my class, all sorts of words would be attached to me. Ching-chong, ching-chong. Slender eyes. Ugly rat. That Chinese girl. That girl with short black hair—the only one most years. That creepy girl who draws dragons.

But for every boy or girl who had said words like that, there would be a few girls who would stick up for me. Don't pay attention to them, they're bullies. Or some boys or girls asked me to draw for them because they had liked my dragons so much. Which didn't really look like dragons at all, more like long creepy snakes that drawn in the sand with the weekly tree trimmings.

I was left out of groups. No one in my class came up to me unless they wanted something. Whenever I tried to fill the gap, to build a new bridge, something always came to break it down. Too many turned backs and awkward looks. Maybe I was the awkward one.

Recess became time to spend by myself. It wasn't as fun anymore.

Then I got hit by a rubber ball. The type they use for dodgeball. Smacked my head hard enough that I fell. A teacher came to me. A few kids asked if I was okay. The kid who had the ball came running over saying they were sorry. They had warned me, they claimed, they said to look out so I could duck or catch it.

But I hadn't heard them at all.

Where had they been when I had lost Spencer? Why do they only come now? I had wanted to shout at them the unfairness of it all. I only nodded and bawled my eyes out.

Someone had brought me to the nurse's office. What's wrong, honey. Where does it hurt. The nurse talked with the others in the office. Why isn't she talking to me. Does she have a hearing problem. How are her eyes. She hears and sees fine. I think her mother said that she was shy. Don't worry about it. She doesn't seem too hurt. She looks like she needs a little rest. See, she is not crying anymore and she is looking bored. Nothing wrong with her. Make sure that she is guided back to her classroom when she's ready. Are you ready to go, honey. I'll be the one to take you. It'll be okay honey.

I know now the concern was genuine. To me back then, they were just words.

GUDELIA VADEN

Violet – The Fairy Princess

If you head East toward the second sparkling star on your right and fly straight till sunset, you will come to River Dale, a magical place where children and fairies play. Among the raspberry bushes, sweet clover and yellow trumpets you will find, Violet, the Fairy Princess.

At five, Violet has golden curls, stands about three feet tall with small hands and feet. When she was born her eyes were a mixture of purple and amber, thus her mother named her Violet the Fairy Princess. She was half midget and half fairy. Violet was more emotional than the other fairies and children that roamed around River Dale. When Violet got angry, her eyes would turn a deep purple. She would burst out crying buckets of crocodile tears. This would also happen if she wanted the swing another fairy had or if she just did not get her way. She was an only child and sharing was difficult for her. Violet could invoke, not only tears, but make the whole city rain tears of anguish. So much, that everyone complained of an impending flood. River Dale welcomed the water to fill its river. Residents wondered where it was coming from and whether or not they would have to be evacuated.

Violet's extraordinary powers came from a golden necklace her grandmother, Queen Rivas had given her not too long ago. Her grandmother, a large, luminous fairy with colorful wings that changed from lavender to cream depending on her surroundings. Her grandmother had the same purple eyes that Violet had, except hers were more intense. She came from the land of Chivas. Fairies ruled there among the lush tropical plants and fragrant flowers.

The necklace was oval shaped and inside was a locket and instead of a photo was the magic potion- fairy dust. All Violet had to do was sprinkle the oatmeal scented fairy dust on herself and right away the fake tears would come in large drops just streaming down her little fragile face. Without it, Violet could not even produce the sounds to cry, such as boohoo!

Violet was an extremely intelligent girl, like her midget father, who was a professor of Botany at University of California, Riverside. He taught her that crocodile tears are drinks for thirsty fairies, thus enabling them to get their needed supply of salt. That nutrient enables the fairies to flutter their wings and fly.

She knew that she was very important to the fairies and that she was doing a good deed by her miraculous necklace. As long as her father could make the potion, she would carry forth the task.

The fairy princess Violet lived happily ever after with her commune of fairies, feeding them juice from her crocodile tears and supplying the city with needed water for the river.

Gudelia Vaden

The Wedding

As a teenager in Planada, California, I was sipping a cup of hot chocolate with canela with my mom in our kitchen. It had rained the night before and the fresh scent of the rain brought her fond memories of when she got married in a cave. I was captivated by her words and wanted to know more. She took a couple of sips of her hot chocolate and I pleaded with her to tell me more about this intriguing story.

In 1927, she was a young girl of 14 when she met Dad, who was 18. While picking nopalitos for her dinner where she lived with her father and step-mother, she noticed Dad on his cream-colored stallion. Their eyes seemed to lock and she swore her heart beat so fast, she would die if she did not meet this handsome tall and slender vaquero. It was love at first sight. She was petite with large dark eyes that sparkled. He plucked a red rose and handed it to her, being careful not to prick her hand with the thorn. Roses grew wild among where the cacti were growing. Mom's family did not approve of him, as he was "a wild cowboy no one could tame." They presumed he would focus his attention on his beloved horse, as was typical of most cowboys, and did not believe he was worthy of their daughter.

The lovers felt they had to keep their feelings a secret from their parents. They wrote love notes to each other and placed them under a rock. Unless you were married, any displays of affection for the opposite sex such as holding hands, embracing, kissing, and even sitting close to each other, were frowned upon.

My mother, Herlinda, continued with her story. She was 15 when my dad, Vicente, proposed to her on bended knee, near the rocks where they exchanged passionate love letters. She accepted as she was mature for her age and very much in love. They wanted to get married in a church, but this was not possible; churches were burned to the ground and Catholic priests murdered by government soldiers.

Many Catholics were in danger of being persecuted for practicing their faith. My parents were very much aware of the beatings and hangings. They knew the government would show no mercy if they caught them. Mother said," What do we do now?" In spite of the almost insurmountable problems, no one could stop these two head-strong lovers from getting married; not parents, not even the government soldiers.

When they finally decided that they would get married in a cave, she expressed she would have liked to wear ribbons and other ornaments; however, she and my father were pressed for time. Mom barely managed to put on a long, ivory-colored dress with matching veil. She had sewn the dress by hand. It was made of cotton with embroidered flowers at the hem. She wanted to look exceptionally beautiful for her wedding day.

It took them three days to find and convince a priest, as priests were being slaughtered. The churches were closed down, so Vicente and Herlinda located a cave. They took off their boots, caked with dust and dirt, upon entering the cave. The priest had to almost whisper, that way no one would be searching for them. It is here in Zacatecas, Mexico, that papá married mamá. After the priest pronounced them man and wife, they kissed. It was the moment they had both waited for to become one body and one soul. Dad was convinced that he had married the most beautiful girl in the world, with her long flowing mahogany hair that went down to her waist. Mom could hardly wait to become truly his, in the eyes of God, and man, and to love him for the rest of her life. She knew she had made the right choice.

The cave had the aroma of how the earth smells after a spring rain. It is not known exactly how long they remained in the cave, but they could have very well spent their honeymoon there. It was all about their safety. When they determined it was safe, they came out; they could not remain in there forever with just some beef jerky and few essentials. They had to move on. They went to live with Father's family on the big ranch where

Mother milked cows, made cheese, gathered the eggs from the chickens, and grinded corn to make tortillas. When Father was not chasing bandits off the ranch, he was herding the cattle and working in my grandfather's Lecheria, a store that sold milk products and sweet bread.

My parents felt like they were the luckiest people to be alive, achieving their mission to get married, despite all the odds that were stacked against them. Standing up to their ideals and beliefs renewed their faith in God. I am grateful for their courage and commitment.

Eventually the Cristeros War, after running its course from 1926 through 1929, came to a halt with the help of the United States. Ambassador Dwight Morrow made peace between Calles (named after President Plutarco Calles) and the Catholic church.

Vicente and Herlinda were married twenty years before they immigrated to Riverside, California with their four children. I was the youngest at almost two years old. After two years, they moved to Planada in the San Joaquin Valley. They shared another fifty years together in Central California, where they raised seven children. Their marriage was based on trust and admiration. Each parent treated the other like they were the most important person in the world. They had so much fondness and love for one another.

I am grateful for the times spent with my mother in the kitchen, spinning tales of her extraordinary life, especially the days when we shared a cup of hot chocolate reminiscing about her most unusual story about her wedding. Her past is my family legacy that will be shared with my husband, my son and daughter, and generations thereafter.

Thomas Vaden

An Ode to Whitney Houston
your fans will miss you; we will always love you

Whitney poised on the stadium
Star Spangled Banner, Home of the Brave
Little did we know that soon thereafter
Her life would end in silent disaster

Her voice clear as a bell
Love songs that caused a swell
In our hearts, a love
That shown from above

We miss her today
Tomorrow afraid
No one to replace
A siren with such grace

Alicia and Kevin paid tribute
A final salute
To the one who left
Our world so blessed

By her presence

Thomas Vaden

Grandpa Bert's Dilemma

There are all kinds of Grandmas and Grandpas. Marie Cook, my grandma, was a strict disciplinarian who had a full-blooded Irish temperament. She was the authoritarian in our household, as well as the cook. And, you did not mess with Grandma's kitchen! She was married to Grandpa Bert, a mild-mannered Dutchman who worked as a head waiter at Bar Les Freres, a high-end French restaurant in St. Louis.

Growing up in the '40's in St. Louis, we never knew we were poor. My three brothers, little sister and I always had food on the table, fresh eggs for breakfast – pilfered from the chicken coops in our backyard – milk, butter and bread delivered to our door from trucks that rumbled down brick alleys, and for our evening supper, grandiose family meals such as Grandma's chicken and dumplings. We did not endure a potato famine like our Irish ancestors, nor did we spend time in long lines – waiting for food – like our parents, who lived through The Great Depression. Our dad had left, abandoning my mom and her five children. But we had grandfather Bert, who loved us and would take us out.

Outside the air was warm and breezy, and the sky was as blue as a robin's egg, with not a hint of rain. The leaves had turned crimson, gold and amber making it a perfect day to be with the grandkids. Fall was Grandpa's favorite season. On a Saturday morning, Grandpa walked down the spiral staircase and saw his grandchildren scrubbing the walls. They had stains on their clothes, their hair needed combing and their faces were soiled brown from cleaning dust and grime. This upset him and he knew he had to do something. He said, "Finish your work kids, and I will take you to the movies."

Our chores completed, Mom cleaned us up and put on a fresh

change of clothes so we would look presentable when Grandpa took us out. Not only did he take us to the movies, but he bought us the biggest bag of popcorn with lots of melted butter. We could also have Snickers and sodas. Grandma wasn't there so we could devour sweets to our delight. After we snickered and laughed at the "Three Stooges," Grandpa was ready to take us to the corner drugstore for ice cream sundaes, my favorite – banana split with a cherry on top. My siblings preferred ice cream cones of chocolate, strawberry and vanilla. We felt as if we were in heaven, savoring all the goodies and licking our fingers. What a sight we were with ice cream all over our faces and cleaned starched shirts.

Grandpa routinely treated us to the movies, and he would not break his routine, even though he knew he would often be in deep trouble with Grandma when he took us home. His black hair dishevelled; his kind caramel eyes appeared worried as he realized he had to face the not so pleasant music. He knew Grandma's light complexion would turn blood red, like the darkest fall leaves; and, she would yell so loud you could hear her all over the neighborhood. After all, she had slaved over a stove making the children a good solid meal and they would not eat, as Grandpa had ruined their appetites. Well, that's Grandpa Bert for you!

Thomas Vaden

Negotiation

She said she had a headache
    And could not perform

I said I had a fever
    For her beauty and charm

I could see in her eyes
    That she needed some space

Her blond hair, her touch
    Gave her a sense of grace

I could offer her Tylenol
    Headache to leave her

What could she offer me
    For my fever?

Thomas Vaden

Truth Simplified

Math is eloquent when simplified
One who understands simplifies
One who does not complexifies

Beauty is truth

Truth is simple

$E = mc^2$

E is for Einstein

E is for Equation

E is for Energy

E is for Eloquence

Beauty is in the laws that govern the Universe

Laws of nature are simple

How eloquent is simplicity

Truth is beautiful!

Alan Van Tassel and Sarah Van Tassel

A Person In My Life

When I was a youngster of about 4, my grandmother was my caregiver during the day. I mostly had her to myself. My mother worked for an attorney in town. His name was Mr. Foot. I guess that was a good name for an attorney. He could really put his foot down in negotiations. My Dad worked as a surveyor. We lived in a small university town that was growing quickly. This town was founded on the barbed wire industry. There were monuments in special places to that industry. The mascot for the high school teams was a bird called a "barb". Our team was always the Barbs.

My grandmother raised six children with her husband on the farm that belonged to the man who invented barbed wire with his partner. Her husband, my grandfather, was a ranch hand. He died at the age of forty of tuberculosis. My mother was the youngest of the six. She was two when her father died. My grandmother made a living for her and her six children working in the big house on the farm where my grandfather worked. Her job was to launder in the basement. She ironed everything: sheets doilies, shirts, underwear.

My grandmother continued that particular skill to the day when she was my caregiver. She would spend her mornings ironing everything made of cloth, including sheets and pillowcases. I used to watch her iron from the other room. She thought I wasn't watching, but I remember her pushing and folding the sheets and pillowcases around the ironing board. There was a rhythm to her work. The cadence of her task was directly related to the timing of the hymns we whistled and hummer.. Very young, I knew many of the hymns from my Sundays and Wednesdays at church. My grandmother didn't attend church, but she knew the melodies by heart. One of her favorites was "In the Garden". This hymn was one we asked our friend, Gene, to sing at her funeral service. It has become a standard at all the family funerals since hers. She used to say that she didn't think she should attend church since she didn't have the money to contribute. I think of her whistling the tunes every time I sing one of her hymns in church. Frequently a hymn from her hymn book will pop in my head. I just hum along as if I was listening to her whistle the tune in the kitchen by the ironing board.

Gramma walked with a significant limp. I am sure she would have had a new hip today, but then those who suffer this malady just put up with the pain. She never complained and never used a cane. She would not take help getting up and down steps. If one of us would try to help her she would wave us away as if we were in the way. She was the helper in our lives.

On days when the weather would allow, I would go out and play in the yard. I was a very curious little guy, so I would tend to wander off. I would go off to other homes in the neighborhood and knock on the door to find out if there were any kids who wanted to play. I would find kids in many homes and we would swing or play tag in their yard. Sometimes they would come to get me. When it was time to come in, my grandmother would step out onto the front stoop and whistle loudly. If I didn't hear it right away, the other kids would let me know that "gramma" was calling. Gramma would keep whistling until I appeared in front of her. If I took too long by her estimation, she would scold me for not coming right away. She would say, "I don't have time for your nonsense."

One of my early memories was the annual spring trip to the cemeteries where we would wash the stones and plant what I knew to be "cemetery flowers" on the graves. In the oldest of the cemeteries there was a hand pump on the well we used to get water for the flowers. On my grandfather's grave, gramma's husband, we would plant one for the head, two for the shoulders, and two for the feet. From the grave sight we could clearly seen the big house where gramma worked all those years. Frequently we would stop there on our way to and from places, get the bucket out of the trunk, and water the flowers. At each stop we would fill the bucket at the well, throw water on the stone and wash it clean. The red marble shone in the sun. We could clearly read "William Columbus Metcalfe 1880-1920." Gramma was a widow for forty-six years. Years later, I brought my three boys to the cemeteries before Memorial Day to wash the stones and plant cemetery flowers. It was a tradition I hope they will continue.

One of the things about a boy that my gramma could not tolerate was dirty ears. If she saw a speck of dirt on my ear she would grab me and take me to the sink to clean my ears. Although she was a very caring person, she was not gentle when cleaning my ears. It taught me a lesson that my ears should always be clean. Some days we would visit my aunt's house who had five boys, all older than me. Her husband "worked at home." At the sight of gramma and me striding up the sidewalk they would all run. Gramma would stand on the front stoop of their house and whistle. Pretty soon we were all lined up by age waiting to get their ears cleaned. Of course, I was first, since I was the youngest. Gramma would grab me by the ear, leading me to the sink in the bathroom. Soon my head was in the sink. I didn't dare say a word. All I could do was groan in fear that my ear wouldn't be there when she was done. Even though my oldest cousins stood as tall or taller than our grandmother, they would comply as gramma reached up and grabbed their ears each in turn. This memory was one we all shared. Years later we would all share this memory of our gramma cleaning our ears and her standing on the front stoop whistling for us to come, get in line and take our ear cleanings like a man.

On special days I would go on a cab ride with my gramma to my mother's office in town. We would sit together in the back seat, watching the cab driver make the turns and stop at the stop lights. I would, of course, chat up the driver. My gramma was sometimes mortified at my questions. "How many kids do you have?" "Where do you live?" "Where do you go to church?" Gramma would hand the driver a silver dollar and he would flip it in the air as he held the door for us to get out. I watched to make sure he caught it. I was sure I would have a chance to pick it up from the pavement. I had no such luck. His eyes were fixed on the shiny silver dollar spinning in the air, all the way up and right back into his hand. He would hold it up and admire it, then put it safely in his pocket.

I learned many lessons in life from my gramma. One was the work ethic. Every day was a productive day for her. Every day she was dressed before breakfast. There was never a time that she would appear at the kitchen table in her robe. She would never complain about her work and she would always have a pleasant smile and a positive greeting even though she was in pain 24/7. I have tried to emulate her positive attitude even though I experience some of that pain she had in her life. Recently I heard from one of my colleagues that it was nice to see me smile when I came to work in the morning. The person talking said it brightens their day to see me cheerful even though they knew my life has had challenges. I know that it's the memory of my gramma that keeps me cheerful even when I have pain and don't feel that cheerful all the time.

Dad had an attitude about my gramma. My mother had four other siblings who lived in town. They would happily come to our house to visit and bring gramma things to wear. His issue was that even though they had fairly comfortable lives, they never contributed to the care of their mother. Gramma had no money. She raised six children on her own, working in the basement of the big mansion in town. She never owned her own house. When my parents were first married and without me, they spent time, caring for her in her rented home. Soon it became obvious that it would be more convenient and economical to have her live with us. It is interesting to note that my grandmother was in her mid fifties when she moved into my parents' home. Now past my fifties and on my way to my seventies, it is ironic to think of my grandmother totally dependent on her daughter and son-in-law for her livelihood. Neither social security or Medicare had been enacted then.

When I arrived, gramma was already installed as a resident in my parents' home. The other siblings made no move to support her. Dad had what he called a burr in his saddle about his issue. He never spoke of it. There was just a quirk in his attitude at times. The tinge in his voice would come out at unexpected moments. Gramma would speak as if she came from the country. She frequently used colloquialisms like "ain't" instead of "am not". Another issue was that Gramma would offer her opinion about things that would come up regarding me and my sister's upbringing and schooling. Dad did not welcome these opinions. Dad had seen the world when he was in the army in World War II. He was an officer. He would frequently tell us that he had found himself in situations where he didn't know which piece of silverware to use first. He said he would watch the others to see what they were doing and just followed. He would instruct us. "The first silverware piece is the one on the outside, then you work your way in". Gramma would listen respectfully and make no comment. If I slipped and said, "ain't", Dad would give Gramma a cold stare. The message was "don't teach my son and daughter to speak as you do!" I felt then that the message was hurtful to her. My sister and I were very careful not to repeat those colloquialisms my gramma used in her everyday language. Personally I loved to hear her stories and her remarks about life and the best way to do things. Gramma knew she was living with us on the good graces of my parents. Gramma did her part, doing the laundry, caring for us kids, providing meals for us at lunch. I would tell my friends that I had three parents. This comment would bring laughter from the kids I ran with. I would explain that my Gramma lived with us. Even though the three of them didn't always agree, for me and my sister, it was true. We had the benefit to be raised by three parents.

1964 is one of the fist elections I remember. Lyndon Johnson was running for his first election as President and Senator Barry Goldwater was the Republican running against him. For some reason my parents were Republicans. My dad would explain that his family lost their farm in the depression. He blamed President Roosevelt. Big business came in and bought out all the farms around the VanTassel farm in South Dakota. The day of the family farm was quickly going its way into the history books. So my parents both voted that year for Senator Goldwater to replace President Johnson. My mother came home from the poles that day with the absentee form for Gramma to sign. Gramma couldn't stand long enough to get in line and wait to vote.at the poles. Mom brought back the ballot from the polling place. Gramma ordered my mother and me out of her room while she voted. When she was done, Gramma called for Mother to come for the ballot which was all folded and enclosed in an envelope to submit to the polling place. Mother couldn't resist looking at the ballot. She looked at the ballot, her arms went right to her waist with the ballot in her hand. "You voted for Johnson," my mother yelled. Gramma was smiling and rocking resolutely in her chair. Mother folded the ballot back up and put it in the envelope, licking the flap and closing it. "We'll just see if this one makes it to the poles!" I got in the car and went with Mom. She dutifully deposited the ballot in the box, waving at the pole workers as she left. Mom dropped me off at our house and headed back to finish out her day at Mr. Foot's office. When I got back in the house, I could hear Gramma singing, "The Old Rugged Cross". I went in her room and asked her why she voted for Johnson. "I want your future to be better than the life I had. I want you to get an education, get a job and support a family. I want you to have health care and a pension. That's why I voted for Johnson."

After that election, Gramma began to get social security even though she had never contributed in her woking lifetime. It wasn't much, but it was a point of pride for her to have some money. Soon after she was gone, Medicare came along. Gramma had taught me a lesson of life. I have been a lifelong Democrat since. I have a pension and Medicare due to many men and women who voted for Johnson in 1964.

In those days the doctor would come to the house. When she was sick, Dr. Telford would pull up in the middle of our driveway in his shiny black two-door Cadillac, get out with his big black leather doctor bag and come to the door. He would never knock. He would just come bustling in the house. He knew where her room was so he would hustle through the house to her room, saying "good evening" or "good morning". When he was finished, he was a man of few words. He seemed to be aware that Gramma's condition wasn't improving.

A major malady of my gramma's was her gallbladder. Dr. Telford advised her many times that she had to get it removed. Then the surgery that would solve this problem would be majorly invasive. Gramma was dead set against this surgery. She would not succumb to the Dr.'s repeated entreaties to get it done as soon as possible. When the problems that come with this malady became unbearable, she finally went to the hospital for treatment. Dr. Telford had to give her the news that she had developed cancer in her gallbladder. They did the surgery the doctor had prescribed years earlier, but it was too late. The cancer had spread all over her body. When she was discharged from the hospital, Dr. Telford advised that Gramma should go in a nursing facility. Of course, she wanted to go home. My mother honored her request. The care she needed was too much for my mother to provide on her own. Mom ended up hiring assistance to come in to relieve her for a few hours of the day. When Gramma was so sick and in pain, they all decided that she should go into a nursing home. The facility was a new one in our city. It was very pleasant and clean. It was called Green Acres. A couple of months and a couple of weeks in the nursing home passed, then she died with all of her children gathered around her. I remember a couple of days before her death was my sister's birthday. Mom took her to see Gramma and have a birthday celebration. I regret I passed on that opportunity to see her in her last days.

I was sixteen when Gramma passed at the age of 78. The funeral was well attended by all her children, grandchildren and great grandchildren. Old friends came to the visitation and told stories about years passed by. I couldn't help but wonder where all these folks had been when she was living. Our friend, Gene

Duncan, who sang hymns on the local radio station, sang "In the Garden" and "The Lord's Prayer" at her service. She was buried in the old cemetery next to the big house where she worked next to her husband. The high school where Gramma, my mother and I attended was in full view of the cemetery. I remember standing there hearing the passing bells ring while we went through the burial service. I looked at my watch to see that I had just missed English class and then soon I would miss French. When it was over, the adults gathered around the stones and talked, reminiscing, discussing Gramma's life and committing to keep the family ties strong even though we all knew that family matriarch was gone. Life would never be the same.

Jose Luis Vizcarra

To Celena

To Celena, a great leader of the written word:

You were created to beautify the world with the most powerful way to beautify the world—books! We appreciate your total commitment to us "scribes" who need your wisdom and guidance.

Our experience is one of passion and creativity pencils, pens, markers, paint brushes, spray paint, lipstick, mascara, and our own blood—when we run out of writing utensils—computers, iPhones, iPads, and whatever we get our fingers on.

Some of us will beg, borrow, and steal to complete our projects. Since we have a full day of activities, positive or not, we go through our days leaving a path to follow or one that is contaminated with useless activities.

Your lessons touch our weak areas and they are like doing physical activities that we have never done before. Those muscles are sore until we use those areas consistently.

As human beings, we are very conscious of our weaknesses and we are afraid to expose our faulty areas. Being published in our book gave each one of us true "scribe pride".

It is so sad to visit a cemetery full of names of people who were totally forgotten. Artists, writers, and those whose evidence behind will never be forgotten. Anyone who picks up our work of art will read our name and refer that creation to others who in turn will be blessed by the author years or centuries when they are gone into the writing center in the sky.

The paper with the flower represents you spreading your seeds of writing all over the world.

Jose Luis Vizcarra

Regardless

Regardless who your parents were
Nobody can pick the parents who they want

Regardless of the care they gave you
Be thankful because they did the best for you

Regardless of the culture you inherited
It took centuries to create, so be proud of it

Regardless of the food that you can eat
There are others who are starving right now

Regardless of the bad school that you attend
Nobody told you that you can't educate yourself

Regardless how you take for granted what you have
one day you might lose them and then you wanted back.

Regardless how you feel superior to others
There are always other who have much more and don't brag.

Regardless how much higher education you have
There are others better educated who didn't go to college.

Regardless how much you possess
I encourage to have much more

Regardless of the fortune that you have
I encourage you to teach others to learn to do so.

Regardless how well you have learned English
I advise you to learn others languages too.

Regardless how smart you think you are
There is wisdom to be acquired

Regardless if you think that you become successful by yourself
You are forgetting those who helped you getting there

Regardless of the problems that you created
Only God can guide you to solve your own mistakes.

Regardless how much you hate to make mistakes
They are the best teacher that we always have.

Regardless of how much texting you do
The only true writing is with a paper and a quill!

BOBBIE WALTERS

A Lonely Visit Saved By Grandmother's Love

The curly headed little girl was perched on a school stool in front of the old upright with her legs dangling, too short yet to reach the pedals, but pounding away with grim determination. She sang at the top of her voice, completely unaware that every creature on the farm was willing her to stop. Only the loyal German Shepherd lying beside her was oblivious to the irritating, strident tones the girl struggled to pull out of the old piano. "She'll be coming 'round the mountain when she comes. When she comes..."

Aunt Aline came into the kitchen for the screen door carrying a bushel basket of vegetables in her arms. The garden was yielding an abundance of produce and everything seemed to be ripening at the same time period. There was little time for conversation and simply no time for the little girl with the screeching voice and sad eyes pounding away at the old Steinway in the alcove.

"Is she still at it? That child does not have a musical bone in her body; even the chickens are nervous at her caterwauling. You might think she would get tired of that racket. She's been at it all morning. Can't you find something else to occupy her?" Aline said to the child's grandmother who was standing at the sink straight stringing green beans.

"She's just a little girl," Grandmother Eunice replied. "She'll get tired soon enough, and when she does I'll encourage her to play on the swing outside. She can wait there for the school bus to return with the other children. I know she's making a racket and it's hard to listen to, but it's somehow it gives her comfort. She misses her folks. A month is long time when you're five. Especially when the other kids are at school; leaving her alone with just that old deaf dog to keep her company."

"I hope they come to pick her up soon," said Aline. "My kids know how to occupy themselves without someone entertaining them all the time. She wants someone to talk to her every minute, and I just don't have the time. Anyway, I hope they finish their business and get back here soon before she drives me crazy pounding that old piano. That child is talentless."

"Don't be so hard on her. She's just a lonely little girl. She has plenty of time to learn to adjust to life's hard lessons. I agree she's not going to be a Beethoven, or a Jenny Lynd, but you have to give her credit for persistence. She surely not a quitter! It's to still too soon to tell whether she will become a butcher, a baker, or candlestick maker. But whatever she becomes she will go at it with gusto. You'll see God has a plan for her he just hasn't revealed it yet. Give her time she's only five," the child's grandmother replied

"Sorry, Mom. I'm just tired and short tempered. This little guy inside of me is making me cross and irritable. Number three isn't any easier than it was with the first two," Aline said, patting her belly and smiling to herself.

The two women continued to work in silence to the screeching background of "She's Coming Around the Mountain." Each lost in daydreams of what the future may bring to those in their care, of both young and old.

BOBBIE WALTERS

A Lonely Visit At Aunt Aline's House

The little blond girl, with Shirley Temple curls, was pounding away on the old Steinway in the alcove just off the kitchen of her aunt's farm house. The old German Shepherd lying on the floor beneath her, raised its head to look up, when her feet accidentally brushed its fur. The child, too short to reach the pedals, was intermittently singing at the top of her lungs or talking to the dog at her feet. She had been perched on the piano stool since the school bus took the other children away at 6:30 a.m.. She would not be six until next school term.

Pounding away with Viking determination and no rhythm, the girl spoke to the dog, Prince, "I love this song, don't you? It means Momma is coming to get me soon. Maybe she won't be driving a wagon, but are Ford is just as good as an old wagon, isn't it?" She continued singing, "She'll be coming around the mountain, when she comes...when she comes..."

Finally, tiring of the song the little girl sat down on the floor next to the dog, and began a serious conversation with him as he stretched out for a belly rub.

"Prince, will Momma bring me a surprise? She said she would. I asked her what my surprise would be, but she said I would have to wait and see. Will it be a big girl-doll and a long wedding dress or a white veil? Cousin Billie Wren has a wedding doll. Will it be like hers? Will she bring me a new coloring book and crayons with lots and lots of pretty colors? There are so many things she could bring me. I wonder what my surprise will be." Bending down to hug the dog, the little girl quietly whispered, "I want Momma to come back soon, so I can go home. I miss my house and my real dog. His name is Freckles, because he has brown spots just like the ones on my nose. He's just a silly little puppy. But, I'm going to train him to do wonderful tricks. Can you come home with me to visit Freckles? Can you do tricks, too? If you don't know how, I will train both of you. My daddy gave me a picture book that shows how to take care of dogs and teach them to turn over, fetch slippers, and catch balls. Will Aunt Aline let you come home with me for a visit? We would have lots of fun and I know you will love Freckles," she said, hugging the dog's neck tightly.

The little girl suddenly wiped a small tear from her eye and quietly confided in the attentive dog's ear, "I'm sad, but I'm a big girl now. I'm not supposed to cry like I'm a little bitty baby. Grandmother told me to sing when I feel sad or lonesome, because it would make me feel good again. But she's wrong. I've been singing all day, but I still feel sad."

"I pray for Momma to get me every day, but she never does. Maybe I'm not praying right. I'll ask Grandmother if I am doing it okay. She knows all about praying. Do dogs have a Jesus to pray to? Let's go find her. She'll know if dogs are supposed to pray like children do. She's a really good teacher. Maybe she'll give us a treat if I asked her real nice and say, 'please.' I've been a good girl all morning and I didn't cry out loud. Not one time!"

JACK WILDE

The Turnout

As a toddler hugs the floor on all fours, the white billowing clouds below slowly creep their way across the ground laid out before me. Abruptly above them, an ominous, shark skin gray color replaces it and silently glides in an opposing direction.

A rumbling of motorcycles slowly grows and as the din reaches its boiling point, all noise suddenly stops. French language drips into both ears. The drip turns into a deluge.

In a black leather vest and tied-off bandana on his head, a man walks to the overlook edge. In English threaded with a thick French accent, he says, "God Bless America." This seems to be a phrase all the French speakers understand, and as they all stare down into the canyon below, they nod in unison—a subtle reminder of how people from afar appreciate the beauty our wide openness has to offer; perhaps better than its own citizens.

Down the middle of the canyon walls, a myriad of brown tones harmoniously run in twists and curves together, like separate music cords brought together to make a symphony; the hues of reds, browns, adobes and whites splash into your eyes. The splash swelling into a flood.

Thoughts turn to miracles, hundreds of thousands, maybe millions, to make this surface as smooth as a child's marble—with only something as soft as moving water.

Like a heavyweight's punch to your nose, you take in the wet mesquite, scrub oak and pines all in one magical breath. Only someone who has visited the desert after a rain understands that if the Southwest had an official smell, this would be it.

The Grand Canyon is just that, but get past its enormity and you'll find many equally as beautiful if you'd only slow yourself down and take in the turnouts once in awhile.

Jack Wilde

The Pacific Slide I

Over the towering coastal range, daylight breaks and the sun appears to rise a little slower than in other places.

Ankle waves gently lap the shore. Latin music hangs in the air and much like a tropical breeze on your sunburnt skin, the sounds cool your soul.

In front of her bayside cafe, a dark-skinned woman rakes the beach sand and anticipates those anchored in her harbor-ita coming ashore for espresso and to catch up on last nights gossip. Their ultimate goal is to beat out the water-taxis bringing the day-trippers and those rewarded for sitting through the entire timeshare sales pitch. Before the woman finishes her pre-tourist duties, all chairs, tables and loungers will come to rest like the crease in a soldier's dress uniform. She knows the cruisers by name and pretends to know each day-tripper, because—before the days end—they, too, will be lifelong friends.

The motor of a fishing panga starts up and idles past. The fisherman reaches a polite distance and he chooses speed over noise. With the ocean waters slowly rippling like a dark silk sheet, it's easy to watch the rollers come towards you. Finally, after a short eternity, our vessel does its anchor dance.

Like the wild west frontier in its day, you can read about it, hear about it maybe even long for it, but the fact remains, it's not for everyone and that's ok. Nothing ever is.

Sailing life along the Pacific Coast isn't like some other better known more exotic locations. Truth be told, I don't think it will ever catch on as such, but somehow I don't think the people here mind at all.

POET-TRY ONLINE

Stephanie Barbé Hammer

Cindi Neisinger

Keto-Tass-Tic

Erica's eyes blinked back tears. As she looked out the window of their new low-carb coffeehouse and bakery, Ke-Tone Kafe.

It's true? Across the street a bulldozer grazed the dirt and a new sign confirmed it. Starbucks coming soon. She read about it in the Malibu Star, but couldn't it have been built on another corner? Of all the corners—Isn't that a running joke somewhere?

She's a take no shit, green eyed, redhead, a little on the thick side, but getting slimmer by the week, on the keto diet. Everyone's heard the word Keto, right? How could you not—It's the current low-carb diet fad. With over one million followers in a FB group called Keto for beginners. Previously, known as, the Atkins diet. It's a sugar free, very low carb, high protein, and lots of high fats —Do you like bacon? Cheese? And butter, butter...on everything! This reduction in carbs puts your body into a metabolic state called ketosis. Ketosis converts fat to energy. Enough of science right? It works.

"Hey! Don't worry so much." Greta tried to reassure her. "Remember why we opened this place— to serve the best damn coffee and cake. And rule the keto world! Right?"

"Fuck ya! Erica wiped her tears away. They've been together five years and going strong. Her wifey.

She had an excuse for her extra weight—their new baby girl. She and Greta, are taking turns making a family. The sperm donor was Greta's first love, Dex. Daisy is six months old, now. In five months, Greta will give birth to a boy, Dylan. They didn't use artificial insemination, either. Dex said, "It was an honor and his pleasure." He sounds like a perv—but, he donated a kidney to his best friend too. Big heart, great genes.

Erica noticed a wet stain on her blouse. And threw a towel over her shoulder, to cover it up. Pumping was her life, her schedule was a little off lately, since coming back to work. Milk overflow. She hated leaving Daisy, with Greta's Mom. But, happy she was safe and loved.

Erica bent down and lovingly, kissed her belly. "Let's get that money babe!" She met Greta at a Tiki bar in Huntington Beach. Black hair and a voluptuous body covered in tattoos. A living, beautiful mural. She smelled like vanilla sugar. It was her first female experience. She tells everyone, I kissed a girl and I liked it.

"Can you believe the line at the door? Wow!" Greta said. „We worked our asses off! This is incredible. Keto friendly is the shit!"

As, she opens to the public. The strong, aromatic scent of Cuban dark roasted coffee, charges through the entrance. The chime of the door opening and closing is so welcomed. Ke-tone Kafe has small chic bistro tables and lounge type couches in the corners. They wanted comfort and ambiance. Check.

"Welcome! Come on in. It's two for the price of one on our bakery items." Greta said.

She is the hostess with the mostest, and very proud of her baking skills. She studied in Paris, France, under one of the best pastry chefs—world renown Chef Hugo Bisset.

Ericka was in charge of making the coffee, ordering and the general bookkeeping. Not so good with people skills. She did have skills in running the coffee grinder and frothing machine— together in a synchronized, whirling like—symphony. They were hoping to hire one part-time employee soon, to work the cash register and table clean up, during the rush hour. Although, Starbucks might squash that goal.

Last week, pictures of their best seller, a sugarless, golden, moroccan cinnamon cake, had gone viral in all the Keto groups, giving them a glimmer of hope. It's made with organic almond flour, served warm in a bowl swimming in some silky Kerry Gold Pure Irish Butter. By 10am, they're sold out. A sugar-free slice of heaven.

"Hey Greta, hurry up with that buttered coffee,—You have me hooked on it girl! I gotta wave to catch, in that brine, called an ocean." Milo said. A big smile and faded-tattooed skin that looks like soft brown leather, he's one of the older, sun loving, surfer dudes that live in this area.

Malibu is a zen place to raise kids, plus, Erica grew up there. She inherited this place from her rich Aunt Viva. She missed her so much, she always smelled like cookies and took her in after she came out to her parents, in high school. They were bible thumpers. No discussion. Bye.

Erica helped her out in her shop, while she went through chemo. Fuck cancer! Her only kids were her fur-babies, two Tri-colored Shih Tzu's, Roxy and Nina. It was a Bohemian boutique, lots of bellowing, oversized dresses—Stevie Nicks-ish style.

When Aunt Viva passed....they remodeled it—into a coffeehouse. They were going to sell it but, Erica met Greta and now they have a family and a dream.

Mid-afternoon, and it's slowed down a bit. Erica was in the refrigerated, backroom taking stock and organizing her collected breast milk baby bottles. She's exhausted from manual-pumping. It's stressful earning her mommy stripes. But, she is hopeful in the near future, to be able to buy an electric pump. Much more efficient.

Greta was busy replenishing the low-carb baked goods. They are a team. She baked, served customers and Erica did everything else. It worked.

In walked a beautiful girl, Tassy, and her entourage. Greta recognized her as the star on a reality show she watches on a popular YouTube channel. It's called Keto-TasTic. Over three-million subscribers. Including her. Erica not so much—she's not into it.

"I can't believe it!"Greta shrieked. She's so gorg. A dark haired Kardashianish type. And well I like girls! I'm so obsessed with her.

"What's going on out there?" Erica yelled from the supply

area.

"Can I have some service here?!" Tassy annoyingly demanded in a high-pitched valley girl voice.

"Like, NOW! Fuck! Do you not know who I am? OMG.... like—I know you've seen my show. Keto-Tass-Tic? Right?"

She had seen it and the transformations were inspiring. Tassy basically has a group of people live in a house for six months and everyone is monitored on the Keto diet. With a big reveal in the end. Hulu has picked it up for an Original Series for next season.

"Thanks for coming Tassy. We watch...., Greta said.

Tassy interrupted. "Stop, OK! What are you a creeper—I'm so sick of people kissing my ass. Now just serve me your best Keto Friendly coffee and a small, tiny piece of that cake that I saw on Instagram—just a crumb, and I'll recommend it on my show. IF, I like it?" She sat down with her pink Louis Vuitton bag. Grabbed her phone and took a selfie, waving Greta off.

"Still a bitch!" Erica mumbled under her breath, fixing her bra, she was leaking milk again, as she closed the door to the supply room. Erica and her go back some years. Both Malibu High cheerleaders, for a few months anyways. Tassy had Erica kicked off the squad for being to fat. She was the squad leader and warned her privately. They couldn't win the championships with a chub. Well, that's not what she told the school board—she lied and said I made a pass at her. I was gay but, not desperate! It was fine, though. It really wasn't her thing.

I have a special recipe for this reality-star, premadonna. She whirled up the milk, frothy and light. Creating a happy face with the foam. She handed it to Greta carefully with a Cheshire smile.

"Here you go Tassy. Our best butter coffee with Keto salted foam on top and a little piece of our famous golden cake." Greta smiled at her.

"Enjoy it! Erica yelled from behind the counter. Tassy didn't recognize her.

Erica thought—It's Keto friendly, and enriched with protein, fat, vitamins, minerals, digestive enzymes, and hormones. Plus, antibodies and lymphocytes to boot! But, Only 4 carbs! Oh! Yes! A skinny drink.

"This is so different....like, salty, creamy, but sweet." Tassy said.

Tassy had a white foamy, boobie milk, mustache—she took another selfie, sending it to her three- million followers. Commenting—Like this is the best salted foam, buttered coffee ever....bitches. I'm here in Malibu, at Ke-Tone Kafe. Get here early if you want a piece of their Moroccan Golden Cake...sugarfree bliss. Like, it's the bomb.

"Better than any Starbucks'. Tassy said, 'I'm going to promote you. Get ready for the rush girlies, when can I bring my crew in? I want you to be part of my show. You're welcome!"

Erica thought, Starbucks, is that all you got? I have to order that electric breast pump! And time to hire our first employee, too.

Go! Ke-Tone Kafe! Go! Ke-Tone Kafe!

A karma lesson in manners. You are what you eat? A boob! Be nice to people. You never know when you will meet up again.

S. J. Perry

I'm Thinking of a Christmas

Which one it was I can't seem to remember.
All I know is it happened one December
When winter winds completely chilled our bones
And glistening sleigh bells rang in jingling tones.

We might've cut a wild tree by a lake,
Or maybe it was just a store-bought fake.
Could be it was a pine with fluffy flocking.
Or we had no tree; each kid had a stocking.

Perhaps we all sang carols 'round the fire.
Maybe we went to church and heard a choir.
That holiday was just so long ago
I can't remember it. I just don't know.

Was it the Christmas Uncle Bill got drunk?
That time we found our gifts stashed in the trunk
Of that old Chevy our folks used to drive?
I must have been just four—or maybe five.

Was it the year the boss gave Dad the bonus
When he bestowed those shiny new bikes on us?
Was it the year the factory closed its gates,
And Mom could pile no feast upon our plates?

Was it before the War on Christmas started,
When Yule celebrations were pure-hearted?
Folks used to know the reason for the season
Before Fox News said Starbucks cups were treason.

I can't remember which Christmas it was.
My memory just seems full of festive fuzz.
It must have been a season filled with mirth,
When we still hoped we could find peace on earth.

RIVERSIDE AT THE RIVERSIDE PUBLIC LIBRARY

with Jo Scott-Coe

CelenaDiana Bumpus

First Clarinet

San Bernardino, CA to Toledo, OH and Back (1985-1986)
Her mother bought her first clarinet that year
before they separated, her to Toledo, and she to San Jose.
The instrument was shiny, wooden and onyx. The young girl coveted
it on first sight, played it in every parade and performance.
Reserving private recitals for her mother. The day her mother
drove the girl to the airport, for summer vacation,
the girl carried the clarinet, cradling it
like a baby. Neither realized she would return
a year and a half later, empty-handed, the music silent.

Bird II

It's my fault you died alone—cold and forgotten
and starving in a dank, dark garage next to a brand
new washing machine and dryer. I knew they drowned
out your weak chirps for help. He said he would
take care of you; instead, he tucked you away with
his dirty laundry—small, dry water dish and
a few scattered seeds in the bottom of a flimsy
cardboard box (your home) did you a fat lot of good
with your beak broken into shards. How long did
he expect to take care of you with your shattered beak
and your broken wing. No veterinarian willing to take you.
No shelter open during the holiday weekend. I should have
snapped your neck when I found you.

CelenaDiana Bumpus

These challenging days...
(No rest for the ___)

even my optimism is suspect
like a yo-yo or a litmus test
    the pH balance rocking like Boris Karloff's pendulum
    and beneath it, tied to the table
        are the jumbled letters of my 50 favorite words

        Why can't I remember their meanings?

my little cousin (she's 6'1") texted me sometime in March (I think)
asking me if I turned 50 this year (she's 5 years younger)
maybe I'll respond in June
    still I'm the reluctant role model
    I married late in life, too (at 37)
    didn't plan on having children (she's childless, too)

  but I'm the wanderer that traded one desert for another
  and what's a dolphin supposed to do in the sand?

Meandering

1.
restlessly—sleepless
my heart longs for an outlet
squeezing out ideas

2.
what's concealed beneath
layers, hiding truth from sun
minute flaws shadowed

3.
idle balloon bops
along hazy striations
plump musical note

4.
Santa Ana clouds
hop blue skies like white bunnies
melting Easter treats

5.
space and time do not
adhere to confines of "now":
unless sun freezes

6.
found medals—letters—
some old photos, while cleaning
house after your wake

7.
confectionary
clouds claim lapin likeness while
mom hunts chocolate

8.
all steps aren't clear paths
to your coveted high rise—
sometimes, they plummet

9.
advice: a humming-
bird—is any sample sweet
enough for some truths?

DEENAZ COACHBUILDER

Chambers of the heart

Lois was out for the first time after having a baby, Reigh,
   now two months old.
"She was the kind of person who would do anything for anybody".
Her two children will never see their mother again.

Ivan Filiberto adored his young son and daughter. They say
   he was very caring of his ailing mother.

Derrick, trying to protect his son Dion from being killed, breathed
his last breath in his arms. A loving family man,
he painted houses and loved to fish and cook.
   His sister Twyla, "cannot understand why…".

Jordan died shielding her infant son from gunfire.
"She was the light of our family, full of heart".
Her husband Andre was killed too, covering them both
with his body. Their little one's fingers were broken.

They were fathers, sons, babies, sisters, friends and lovers
   even a grandfather,
               on an ordinary day,
making plans for the evenings,   texting friends,   kissing loved ones,
shopping to get ready for the first day of school.
All gone,
     in the time it takes a bullet
               to meet its target.

Do not mourn any more.

Our drained bodies are encrusted
  with stagnant pools of tears
that seep into this beloved country.

Do not spread flowers along these sacred scenes
  for there are not flowers enough to
cover the blood.

Is that your heart that bleeds?
O close shut that chamber
  so you may survive.

The nation experienced back-to-back mass shootings in El Paso and Dayton on August 3rd and 4th, 2019 respectively, that left over 30 dead and many wounded.

Poem of the Month, June 15, 2019, published by Magdalena Rustomji.

DEENAZ COACHBUILDER

Those Numbers

Way into the seventies
I said, matter-o-factly
with acceptance,
not resignation.

Currents humming
around me
subtly change.

They stumble
unsure, wondering
encircle protectively
let me take your plate
may I help you?
warm-hearted
instant unearned veneration.

60, 70, 80
fleeing decades
lived ungently
a brimming river
of lucent shells,
some broken, some whole
that hold life's treasures
stretching to the stars
with scattered moments
in between
of spoonfulls of dessert.

When I step
into eternity
it will be
with curiosity
unencumbered
by numbers.

Until
that crossing
let me be

age less.

DEENAZ COACHBUILDER

Grace

Frenetic humanity and mechanical contrivances
whirl alone Mumbai's toro fare.
Double decker buses come to a screeching halt.
Hard at work, taxis of varied colors and sophistication, cars,
scooters and motorcycles compete to occupy any vacant space
as pedestrians cross at will, playing a tempting game with fate.
Like a wayward child that refuses to obey,
the traffic saunters at a snail's pace, and will not quicken.
Wayside shops are filled with flowers and toys,
street food vendors occupy the narrow pavement,
tempting passersby with the aroma of spice and the sizzle of heat,
while the venerable cobbler sits on his mat, immersed in his trade.

A little bit
    of sunlight
        angles
  its way
through the tall buildings packed familiarly together.
Caught in its beams is a single white butterfly,
beating its large wings in an unconcerned fashion
fluttering up and then across,
                and in a heartbeat,
                        is lost
    in the immersing dust.

Previously published in *Parsiana*.

Deenaz Coachbuilder

Fire and Earth

Stripped of beauty
on denuded hillsides
they stand
mute
bare arms reaching towards
unheeding smudged skies.

Just yesterday blue spruce
fluttered supple eyelashes at wooing birds
rustling Douglas fir sang a resonant summer chorus
while variegated wild fruit hid in
clumps of foliage that dotted
Shasta-Trinity's sacred forest landscape.

Mercurial fire
healer and destroyer
knows no favorites.
It slays suddenly   without mercy
smiting old and young
turning rainbow hues into charcoal.

Earth patiently weaves new garments
a bride designing her trousseau
silk and taffeta for the night
light cottons for the spring days ahead
while the sun bursts juvenile seed,
gleaming jewels for her hair.

The Hirz and Delta wildfires burned vast areas of California's Shasta-Trinity National Forest in the summer of 2018.

Previously published in *Quill and Parchment.*

Carlos E. Cortés

Ode to Baron Scarpia

    Opera goers are supposed to hate Baron Scarpia
The arch villain of Giacomo Puccini's *La Tosca*
The Hannibal Lecter of grand opera

Scarpia, the bloody, tyrannical Chief of Police
Runs a reign of terror over Rome, 1800
    Arresting
    Torturing
    Mutilating
    Killing
Lusts after singer Floria Tosca
    Intent on seducing her
    And if that doesn't work
    Dedicated to raping her
Desecrates a cathedral Mass
    Singing about his lust for Tosca
    Drowning out the devout who are extolling Jesus
    Entoning, "Tosca, you make me forget even God"
Lies unrepentantly to Tosca
    Promising to spare her imprisoned lover
    In exchange for her body
    While surreptitiously ordering his execution
    On the roof of the Castel Sant'Angelo
    Which Laurel and I visited
    During our last trip to Rome
Before dying at the hands of Tosca
    Stabbed to death as she spits out

"This is Tosca's kiss."

But I don't go to the opera to love or hate
I go to
    Observe the spectacle
    Soak up the ambience
    Revel in sonority

The first times I heard Puccini operas --
La Boheme and *Madame Butterfly* --
I enjoyed them

But once I heard *Tosca*
I was riveted by its
    Darker tones
    Pulsating rhythms
    Sumptuous musicality
    Unrelenting emotion
    Pervasive evil

Now every time I see it
I become increasingly envious of Scarpia's
    Ability to enthrall audiences
    His voice soaring above the gorgeous Te Deum
    That culminates Act One

So in my next life I want
    To be blessed with a rich baritone voice
    To be able to sing like Scarpia
    To actually play Scarpia
    To hear the audience shouting "bravo"
    As they salute my villain from hell

Carlos E. Cortés

Gratitude: The Life of Carlos (With Apologies to Eric Idle)

What did our parents ever do for us?

They raised us in a nice home.

O.K. But except for raising us in a nice home, what did our parents ever do for us?

They gave us a good education.

Well, except for raising us in a nice home and giving us a good education, what did our parents ever do for us?

They took us on fun trips.

Sure, but except for raising us in a nice home, giving us a good education, and taking us on fun trips, what did our parents ever do for us?

They always had lots of music and books in the house.

All right, but except for raising us in a nice home, giving us a good education, taking us on fun trips, and having lots of music and books in the house, what did our parents ever do for us?

CARLOS E. CORTÉS

Out Of Order

Mom screwed up, big time,
when she got lung cancer
   and died
while Grandma was still alive.

Mom screwed up, big time,
not just because she smoked
   two packs a day
   for fifty years
she screwed up, big time,
because she died
while Grandma was still alive
   not in the proper sequence.

Which meant that Grandma
had to watch her daughter die
   before she did
   after a year of agony
   wasting away
   increasingly bitter
   saying terrible things
   things about Grandma
   things she had never said before
   things she didn't have
     the time
     or will
     or energy

   to take back
leaving Grandma to go on,
   alone
   disconsolate
   thinking about her only child
   wondering
why hadn't they passed on in the proper sequence?

Laurel Vermilyea Cortés

The Secret Life of Office Workers

"Laurel (la-oo-rél), I have known you for twenty years and I've never seen you angry."

"Really."

It interests me because as a Spanish woman I am used to demonstrations of anger, but you always stay the same. You are always smiling or laughing."

"Really. Maybe that's why they call us seecretaries, because we can keep things like that secret."

"You are an Office Manager, not a secretary."

"Not much difference…"

"Oh yes! And I've never seen you get angry with your staff."

"Really."

"I've been watching you closely through all kinds of chaos, and I've never heard you raise your voice."

"Well, no one has the right to yell at anyone. That's my credo."

"And yet, many people scream at you. How many professors have raised their voices to you?"

"All but one of you, and that man never steps foot into the office."

"And yet you remain composed."

"There is an alternative interpretation of my steady demeanor."

"Ah, yes? What is it?"

"Perhaps in all these years you have never seen me when I am not angry."

"You're funny."

"Am I?"

Laurel Vermilyea Cortés

On Being Laurel…And Yanny

In the 1937 classic movie melodrama, Stella Dallas, the heroine is a millworker's daughter who catches the eye of one of the mill executives, and they marry. Soon they have a child named Laurel, but the marriage fails because Stella is not "his kind." She gives up her daughter to her husband so that the girl can be "properly" raised and educated. The film ends with a teary-eyed but proud mother watching Laurel--from the sidewalk outside--as she exchanges vows with a perfect handsome rich man. Stella walks away in triumph, knowing that her wrenching sacrifice has paid off for her child. Barbara Stanwyck plays Stella to the hilt, leaving not a dry eye in the movie house.

I tell you this to explain why baby girls born in that era to fans of that movie were named after Stella's daughter. In 1953, there were three Laurels in my sophomore class of 156 students. Never a Laurel before that class. Never a Laurel afterwards. Hooray for Hollywood!

* * * *

I attended Oceanside-Carlsbad Union High School. Because my last name started with V (Vermilyea), I sat in the last row of my Social Living class, taught by one of my favorite teachers, Mr. Barnes. A newcomer sat beside me, named Bill Petrie--long and lanky and hilarious. Together we had much fun back there against the window—the occasional scowl on the face of our teacher warned that we were "cruisin' for a bruisin'."

One day, my friend Laurel Higgins made her rounds gathering the daily attendance sheets from the classes. Opening the door behind our teacher, she reached in to claim the paper just as Mr. Barnes screamed at me, !!!!!LAUREL!!!!! My poor namesake, taken by surprise, burst into tears. As our abashed leader ushered her out to the hallway to calm her down, the class went into hysterics. Mr. Barnes was none too happy with Bill (he was his basketball coach!) and especially me; he separated me from my day-brightener…I mean permanently!

As for Laurel Knott, we each vowed to marry a man named Hardy. I would be Laurel Ann Hardy and she would be Laurel Knott Hardy!

* * * *

All my life I referenced Laurel and Hardy when people called me Lauren, Laurie, Lara, or Laura. That worked until about 20 years ago, when a young man responded "Oh yeah, 'Who's on First!'" Because that was Abbott and Costello's famous baseball bit, it was clear that the jig was up on Laurel and Hardy. Painful. I had to start spelling my name!

But I never had to explain or spell my name in Latin America, where the Spanish pronunciation of my name is phonetic--La-oo-rél--with the accent on the last syllable. That helped when I was a Spanish major at San Diego State and again as I spent my working life in the Department of Literatures & Languages at UC Riverside.

* * * *

Laurel can be a surname. In films, Stan Laurel immortalized it as such, but even Marilyn Monroe played a Lois Laurel (always called Miss Laurel) opposite Cary Grant in the funny movie Monkey Business. She portrayed an eager secretary with no typing, shorthand or filing skills. She didn't need them.

* * * *

According to the Merriam-Webster website, the word laurel is among the top 30% in look-up popularity. It comes from (laurus nobilis) the name of a shrub or tree whose leaves--also called bay leaves—were bent into a circle to crown an Olympic champion in Ancient Greece. The word is usually used in the context of crowning or honoring.

* * * *

In May 2018, a student named Katie Hetzel was assigned to write down the meanings of a list of words in her World Literature class at Flowery Branch High School in Georgia. She turned to Vocabulary.com. Looking for the word laurel, she came across an audio/video posting, but seeing the word laurel, she instead heard yanny.

Ms. Hetzel copied the posting and took it to friends, some of whom also heard yanny while others heard laurel. It became a great source of fun at Flowery Branch, and eventually got into the hands of a student named Roland Camry who posted it to Reddit. The meme was picked up on Twitter by Cloe Feldman, a popular YouTuber with over 670,000 subscribers. Then it went viral and global!

The easiest way to explain the phenomenon is this: those who hear high frequencies often hear yanny, while those who don't may hear laurel. As we age and lose the ability to hear sound at a higher frequency, we probably will hear laurel.

The original recording had been commissioned by Vocabulary.com in 2007 as part of a 200,000-word project. Its co-founder, Marc Tinkler, sought out opera singers to speak into his microphone set-up. He wanted speakers trained, as opera singers are, in IPA--the International Phonetic Alphabet. This training prepares singers to enunciate words in languages they do not know. Tinkler hired a member of the original Broadway cast of CATS named Jay-Aubrey Jones. Mr. Jones recited 60,000 words as they came up on his laptop. One of those words was laurel. It was his recording that Katie Hetzel heard eleven years later--except that she heard yanny!

* * *

One day toward the end of May of 2018, I was perusing headlines on my tablet when I came across Laurel? Or Yanny? Naturally, I hit on it, and found an audio/video posting asking which one of those words I heard. I heard yanny. I thought it was very funny, and mentioned it to my daughter Merrit. Her response? "So that's what's going on!"

Living very close to the Pechanga Casino, Merrit drove down Temecula Parkway Drive every day to the school where she teaches. One of the housing developments along the Parkway has a long and wide sign proclaiming LAUREL CREEK. But the LAUREL had recently been covered with an equally-large-lettered YANNY. My daughter assumed that some new developer had taken over the place and renamed it YANNY CREEK. Now she knew better. We had a good laugh over that.

* * * *

As a Lakers' fan, I watch the Tuesday NBA games on TNT. On the Inside the NBA set sits the moderator, Ernie Johnson--the only man in the world who can tame the commentators Shaquille O'Neal, Kenny (The Jet) Smith, and Charles Barkley into some coherence.

Soon after I talked to Merrit, I turned on TNT. Ernie was saying: "Before we talk basketball, let's get this laurel/yanny thing out of the way." He asked them to listen to the now-famous recording.

"What do you hear?" Shaq heard a combination of laurel and yanny. Ernie heard laurel. Kenny heard laurel. Charles heard… donut. There was laughter and cacophony. "You can't hear donut, Chuck!!! Let's try it again." They played it a second time. This time, Shaq heard yanny. Ernie and Kenny heard laurel again, Charles heard… donut! Everyone in the whole studio now yelled and screamed at him.

Finally, to get the program back on track, Ernie confessed that the engineers had "played" Charles, (as usual) by piping donut into his ear pod. The program went on with basketball--sort of.

* * * *

On voting day, I beat the crowd to the Riverside Water District Office, arriving bright and early to cast my votes in the important 2018 Primary Election. Several polling districts shared the large community hall, and I walked past the other tables to the far side of the room, encountering four young women, barely half-awake. "What is your name?" "Cortés. Laurel... not Yanny."

The millennials erupted into laughter and chatter. Turning to my polling desk to vote, I could hear them in loud and animated discussion about when they heard about laurel/yanny, which one they heard and why they thought it happened. I left them wide awake and having fun. Walking to my car, I felt that I had fulfilled my civic duty, in more ways than one!

* * * *

I once had a friend who tried to write a rhyming poem to me. He was stymied in his effort to incorporate moral, immoral, and (yikes!) oral into his more elevated sentiments--not much else rhymes with Laurel. He wrote a prose poem instead.

When I look back over my eighty years of being tyrannized by my name, I'm really grateful. It's been fun! But I am now called by a name I cherish more than my birth name; I'm now known as Grandma Lolo! Believe me, when I hear that name called out, my heart takes flight!

Nan Friedley

Notes Are Still There

My little fingers
stretched over black and white keys
plodded through Rhapsody in Blue
for beginners, plunked erroneous
notes in largo tempo.

"It's an F#", he yelled from the kitchen.
How could he pluck
the note I should have played
from his musical mind?

He carried the gift
of songs in his head.
Cincinnati Music Conservatory
groomed him for success
to take his talent on the road.

But he took a different path
found a dependable job
nothing to do with pianos
nothing to do with creating music.
He got married, had two kids
(I'm the one who needed that F#).

Piano would always be a part of him
even if only part-time.
Using his gift of perfect pitch

he tuned pianos with felt strips and hammers
joined like-minded guys in a quartet
drummer, bass, and clarinet player
featured music from the 40's, songs like
Stardust and Paper Doll for
couples swaying on the dance floor
Saturday nights.

His band buddies are all gone now.
He forgets what he had for breakfast
forgets that he ate breakfast
forgets where he is and why he's there.

But he remembers
how to play those nostalgic tunes
medley of memories
notes are still there.

Nan Friedley

Losers

I'm a Big Kid Now

Fell out when I bit into a taffy apple at
Trunk or Treat. Took long enough
been wiggling it for a week.
Best friend Gary lost his first one last year
just in time for his first grade picture.
Mine was on the bottom, gross root attached, left
a gigantic bloody hole.
Can spray water like a fountain…so cool.
Eat corn off the cob and applesauce
brush one less. Fairy paid me $5.00.
Need to wiggle others.

Smooth

Fell out gradually, thinner as I got fatter
noticed hair in the shower drain, hair in
combs, hair everywhere except my head.
Empty spaces appeared at my temples, in back
where yarmulkes are worn.
Tried Rogaine hoping to sprout seedlings
fill in the smooth, empty spots.
Brown thumb left a barren scalp.
Doing the inevitable "comb over"
wearing baseball hats for Dodgers and
Angels and Yankees and Cubs and Padres.

Sticky Notes

Fell out, but I try to hang on by
writing labels on sticky notes
tags to identify rooms, furniture, tools.
Google when I can't think of a word
the name of that "thingy"
that "thingy" where cold things live.
Find keys in the freezer and
ice cream in the cupboard
forget how to make coffee
how to start the computer
write a check
tell time
remember.

NAN FRIEDLEY

Triple Double Feature

Hillcrest Drive-In (1963)

balmy Friday night in July
gravel parking lot
one spot left on the front row
lighted playground
kids on swings and see-saws
shadowed on jumbo screen
windows cranked down
speaker hangs precariously
fuzzy sound reverberates
tethered to a nearby post
dotted with used gum
station wagon back seat down
wearing Flintstone's pj's
popcorn in butter-stained paper bags
thermos of super sweet
cherry Kool-Aid
long before final credits
roll, I dream of flubber
slept through the best
of The Absentminded Professor

East 30 Drive-In (1969)

carload of seven teenage girls
"two for one" night

six in seats, I'm in the trunk
take turns at the refreshment
stand, swat gnats
oily French fries
cook in baskets
bags of buttery popcorn
wait under warming lights
sticky counter, coke syrup blobs
greasy pizza and pop
in a cardboard box
flirt with boys in white pick-up
movies on the marquee
Midnight Cowboy and The Wild Bunch
both rated R
I hope we see Dustin Hoffman naked

Blackford County XXX – (1973)

Saturday, date night
college kids jam entrance
cars spill out on State Road #1
two lane highway
stretches to Hartford City
cows moo in nearby fields
Budweiser local boys in trucks
Sigma Chi bros brought
Schnapps to chug
snippets of intercourse and
blowjobs interspersed in
Tom and Jerry cartoons
XXX double feature

Deep Throat followed by
The Devil in Miss Jones
banana and water hose and
snake, oh my
I didn't know you could do that
theater security with flashlights
check rocking cars
steamy windows
life imitating XXX art

Nan Friedley

@ Her

I watched through slats
of plantation shutters
across the street

he's @ her again
picking @ her
pointing his finger @ her
yelling @ her
pulling @ her hair
yanking @ her arm
grabbing @ her neck
laughing @ her

she should hit back @ him
she should call the cops
she should leave him
she should…

I heard the pop

now she's @ my door
seeing her, up close
bruised, defeated
a toddler @ her side
@ a loss for what to do
next

@ least I can call the police
@ least I can tell them
what I saw

I should have done it before

Christina Guillén

La Hada Orange Blossom

> *Grown men can learn from very little children for the hearts of the little children are pure. Therefore, the Great Spirit may show to them many things which older people miss.*
>
> —Black Elk, Oglala Lakota Sioux

Once upon a time, before there was 'make-believe' and there was just 'believe,' there sat the most brilliant kingdom known for its orange trees. The oranges were far more vibrant than we have today. Some grew in rows, others scattered about in the gardens of the simple-loving folk. All the oranges of the land were sweet and their scent wafted for miles at the first sign of spring.

Their fruit began green as limes. You would never guess they were oranges. You would hardly be able to convince a child that the green fruit would one day turn orange. And yet one day always came and up and down the lots of trees were dotted with the most brilliant oranges you'd ever seen.

In fact, on one very special day many moons ago, most likely the most spectacular orange season of all, it happened that a couple ultra-orange oranges fell to the ground before the orange pickers came to work.

One of the oranges was quickly torn to bits by crawlies and hungry little flies while the other stayed in perfect shape with an extraordinary orange glow about it.

And would you believe it was from this glowing orange that a small crack appeared? That something absolutely remarkable happened? Why, tiny little hands felt their way out and split the orange in half and out came a girl!

Of course this was no ordinary girl, she had extraordinary features to begin with, a very beautiful shimmering orange tint to her skin and a set of shiny wings folded on her back. Her youth and purity of her heart made her the youngest, wisest creature on Earth.

She stretched her arms and yawned. She shook her wings and smiled a lazy smile, as though waking up were the most delicious thing she'd ever done.

When she opened her eyes they were the most beautiful emerald green you'd ever seen. They were wide and wondering. She beheld the leaves, branches, and oranges all around her and smiled because she knew them to be her mother.

Although her mother couldn't speak with sound she knew she was saying "good morning."

"Bienvenido, abuelita niña. You are the one and only hada of oranges," her mother seemed to say in another way. "I have decided to call you La Hada Orange Blossom for your hada wings and the sweet scent you will forever carry on your skin."

Slowly and carefully, being just born and all, La Hada Orange Blossom walked to the trunk of the tree. She snuggled into it with cheek and arms to say thank you.

"I meet you in the place where thanks does not exist and yet I am honored by the gesture. May you emerge from the shade of me and show yourself to your father. He is very warm and happy to see you. It is because of him that you have the desire to walk and snuggle."

"And you mama, will you stay here?" La Hada Orange Blossom asked.

She seemed to hear Mama Orange Tree chuckle with delight. "My dear, I do not have legs as you so elegantly do. I cannot leave this spot. But do not worry I enjoy where my roots are settled and am happy to watch you take life and send you on your adventures. Perhaps you will return from time to time to tell me of them?"

"Of course mama, of course, I will!" La Hada Orange Blossom giggled with cheer and kissed her dear mother's dainty green leaves.

"Goodbye mama," she said as she hopped and fluttered her wings.

Mama Orange asked Abuelo Wind to gently shake her so that she could wave goodbye to her only orange hada girl.

Smaller than an orange, little Hada Orange Blossom, made her way from the dappled shade to the sunlit earth and patches of grass.

She felt a great warmth overtake her. Her skin prickled with delight. It was the hug of her father blessing her.

"Papa! It is you! Hello, Hello! I am your daughter Orange Blossom."

Papa Sun spoke without words and Orange Blossom knew just what to do. She closed her eyes and opened her heart and all that she was that you could not see listened deeply.

Papa Sol stroked her face with warmth and said, "Bienvenido abuelita niña, wise joy, how good it is to see you and shine upon you. Welcome to the world!"

"It is beyond lovely to meet you. Thank you Papa for the desire to move. There is so much to do and see! Perhaps you can teach me something this morning, I was only just born and am very eager to learn."

Padre Sun smiled, she felt his warmth travel all the way to her belly to tickle her. "Oh, what things you will learn corazoncita…"

"What? What will I learn Papa?"

"The first thing you may learn is simple. May you go from place to place to do this. May you learn what your senses are good for. May you look with your eyes, hear with your ears, smell with your nose, taste with your mouth, touch with your fingers, and most important, feel with your heart. This is how you may grow to love this world. Perhaps you'll tell me about it from time to time?"

"Of course I will!" she said with so much happiness filling her chest she could hardly stand it. She felt Papa Sun's light dancing. "Apa,' will you stay here?"

"Yes mi'ja, all day I will stay here to watch over you and fill you with joy."

Later, when Papa Sun gave way to dark night sky, not even the moon was out for La Hada Orange Blossom to meet—but the stars, oh my, the vast many stars.

Orange Blossom simply stared and stared. "What wonders, this world!" she marveled. Then it appeared a star winked right at her. So what did she do but wink back!

"Hello bella luz, who are you?" Orange Blossom asked.

Star seemed to chuckle for her newness to life, "I am Hermana Star, dear one. Who are you?"

"I am La Hada Orange Blossom and I'm going to learn many things and have many adventures as Mama and Papa say."

"Isn't that fantastic! I'm sure the Hada People are excited to meet you."

"Hada People? How wonderful! The world must be brimming with friends!"

"Why yes, there is Hada of Strawberry and Hada of Pineapple, Coconut, Chocolate, and even Peanut!"

"Oh! I'm shaking with happiness!"

"Perhaps you will tell me about them from time to time? That would delight me so. I will sparkle on and on throughout the night with gladness for you."

"Yes Hermana Star, I will tell you about all the people I meet and all the fascinating adventures I have," Orange Blossom beamed, folding her tiny hands under her chin.

"Gracias pequeñita, thankfulness wraps my heart in flowers. I offer you my blessing and a blessing on behalf of all Star People who will also wink away at you."

"Oh you are so beautiful inside and out! Thank you!" Orange Blossom said nearly out of breath with excitement. "What a wondrous happy feeling all around."

Hermana Star twinkled and said, "Now it is late preciosita, may you sleep upon the soft earth."

"Oh how will I ever sleep now?"

"Forgive me pure heart, it's my fault that you're excited so. May you go to where Hermano Gopher has dug out his hole—oh forgive me, you don't know Gopher! He is friendly too, you may see in the morning. He is sleeping now but you may lay upon the earth he has loosened making a most comfortable bed. And I'll be here sparkling over you with my lovelight.

La Hada Orange Blossom was filled with affection for Hermana Star and so excited for the new day ahead that she could hardly lay herself down to sleep, let alone stop staring and smiling at her friends above. She went to Hermano Gopher's pile of earth and when she climbed to the top it was like a nice abuela lap, so soft her body sank into it right away.

After a few moments something very kind happened. Very quietly and very gently, Abuelo Viento blew over her with his warm breeze tucking her in. Although they hadn't officially met, she felt he must be most gracious and grand. He invited Orange Blossom to feel quite cozy and comfortable indeed. She yawned, wiggled her wings and toes, and looked up.

She gazed into the light of Heaven until her eyes became so overcome with warm heaviness she couldn't keep them open. She closed them and felt such love feather her heart. Her chest lifted, it was bliss to breathe in the night sky of sparkles.

From far away she could feel Mama loving her. And from a great distance she could feel Papa loving her too, and all the little bright hermanas of luz.

The smell of Orange Mama's familiar fragrance wafted to her a sweet lullaby and she listened to pretty little songs of the other friends she guessed she would soon meet. Her heartbeat pulsed with thanks and she sighed a happy sigh.

Then like a shooting star streaking through the night sky, she remembered about the other hadas. She smiled in the soft Abuela Ground and soothing Abuelo Breeze. Orange Blossom was the happiest hada girl in all the wide wonderful world.

The End

Christina Guillén

Everybody Okay

You have to look deeper, way below the anger, the hurt, the hate, the jealousy, the self-pity, way down deeper where the dreams lie, son. Find your dream. It's the pursuit of the dream that heals you.

—Billy Mills, Oglala Lakota Sioux

There is a small boy in my bedroom. He grabs my hand and squeezes with desperation. I allow him to squeeze as hard as he needs. I tell him I'm sorry. He pulls me outside into the sunny garden and becomes a white rabbit. He is the gift of ulcerative colitis.

There is a doll dangling in the kitchen window. He looks like Dracula with black hair and cape. He will be as strange as he needs to be. I am afraid, but I go to him, my song rising in my throat. My body floats, my back touches the ceiling. A group of Native voices sing to a drum. My feet stomp the air to the beat.

At my side on the couch sits an angry faced woman. My song tries to rise, but I am paralyzed. I sing in my head. The woman makes distorted faces at me. I refuse to slip into fear. I give her my song in my mind. The woman steps into the center of the room and disappears. Her clothing becomes a child's white dress. It floats in shining light.

I feel a deep rumbling in the bedroom. It shakes my being. My voice and I are paralyzed. Two laughing children in the in-between run and hide. I conjure my song from the heart of me and push it through the heavy weight of fear. First the older boy comes to me, then the younger, eyes wide with longing. They sit at my side and on my lap and watch me sing.

I approach a single stall public bathroom. I push the door open. Something is preventing the door from opening all the way. I look behind the door. Someone is standing there. He is wearing a black hooded cloak. I take a deep breath and unwrap the cloak. I see a small child lowering his face. He is the innocent heart of darkness.

ROBIN LONGFIELD

1964 (After Weldon Kees)

1964
The Hi-Fi turned up loud—
"Tell Me Why"
Shakes the walls
Of my cousin Judee's bedroom
In Gardena—

In the dining room,
Ice cubes clink
In highball glasses,
Our parents debate—
Goldwater vs LBJ
Dodgers vs Giants
Ford vs Chevrolet.

In the living room,
A Zenith Television
In its fashionable cabinet,
Shows pictures of a war
Far away—
No-one pays attention
To the somber announcer—

No one pays attention
To 4 subteen cousins—
Judee, Jeanette, Catherine,
And me,

Pretending to be Beatles—
Reading fan magazines,
wishing on stars—
for stars.

In this, our Eden,
Our paper-fortunes
Never told
The lives that lay ahead—
The parents
And siblings
Vanished, vaporized
By drugs and drink,
Mental illness,
slights real or imagined

Our inheritance,
Were memories
Real and imagined,
Reduced to boxes
Of their own—
More contained,
Confined,
Than the television
In its cabinet.

What never left us,
Was 1964,
The hi-fi playing loud—
"Tell Me Why"
Shaking the walls
Of Judee's bedroom

In Gardena—
The hi-fi playing loud—
"Tell Me Why" "Tell me whyyyy"
The hi-fi playing loud—-
1964
The hi-fi playing

Robin Longfield

Bags

Red and blue tents line Gower Street in Hollywood, under the 101; a dark, dank, refuge of the lost by design and the lost by systems that failed them. Visibly invisible, their lives contained in plastic bags piled high, spilling out of tents, overflowing, in bockety-wheeled grocery carts. Bags on their backs, bags on feet that navigate an existence without maps, without GPS, without a plan beyond surviving another day. Existence by experience, instinct; by the voices, by services rendered or received. Bags that patch the tents, bags in the place of tents. Bags in place of hats or winter coats. Bags filled with rats, scratching, scavenging; bags plastered against chain link fences, in gutters. Bags and baggage, this unending posada; through streets of golden piss, the caravan continues, beneath glimmering, shimmering lights from high above them, false angels of mercy guide them on ; always on, moving on, bags and baggage. Deliverance comes in bags, body bags, unclaimed baggage, the county cemetery, a year, instead of a name. In a far away town, a mother, a sibling, a spouse, sit with bags filled with memories, filled with hope, with baggage of their own. Bags and Baggage; the broken circle grows larger, the night sky grows dimmer—where is the North Star, that can lead them all home?

ROBIN LONGFIELD

Before Blue

Before "Blue",
We roamed in sunshine
Down canyon trails,
Sang songs to seagulls,
Dreamt of our own
Nights in the city—
Those colors waltzing in time—

From our canopy beds,

We saw Sistowbell Lane,
Mornings in Morgantown,
And declared
Which Canyon Lady we were—

I aspired to be Annie
Those cats and babies
Around her feet,
The baker of brownies—
It was enough
Cats and babies,
Brownies baking—

But you,
You had already written
Cactus Tree
Years before—

That laundry list
Of doomed suitors
And you
So busy being free—

A prelude
None of us envisioned

When we heard "Blue"
All we wanted
Was to feel, the way you felt,
To feel your words
Inside us
Like breath
In and out, through our skins,
Through the crowns of our heads
And into the universe,
An energy
Acommunion with you—

You said "love is touching souls"
And how you touched ours,
A case of you
Would never have been enough

We needed to feel,
Because we did not know
Anything
Beyond prom night
And our canopy beds—
Nothing
Of the eternal dance

Between joy and sorrow,
How what was lost
Might never return,
How all good dreamers

Do end up
Someday
In those dark cafes.

We are older now
And you are 75,
Your Black Crow wings long gone—
Don Juan's reckless daughter
Home to roost.
We too
Have looked at life
From both sides now,
And give our daughters
Knowing glances
But no words—
Like you
They follow their own
Refuge of the Roads

SAN BERNARDINO AT THE ROWE BRANCH OF SAN BERNARDINO PUBLIC LIBRARY

with Allyson Jeffredo and Romaine Washington

Alben Chamberlain

On The Borderline

On a sunny day I went for a walk and
 thought to cross the borderline.
When I arrived at that mark on my map,
 nothing was there to find.

Barring the roadway were barriers, armed
 guards, and drug-sniffing dogs.
Customs agents on both sides were taking
 in revenue like insatiable hogs.

I walked up to a tall man just standing
 there with his gun.
I smiled at him and asked, "What are you
 protecting us from?"

"Many terrible people over there wish to
 bring drugs into our land."
I replied, "Would they be trying so hard if
 there wasn't such a demand?"

"There are hordes of impoverished people
 who wish to cross to get a job."
I said, "Would they still be coming if our
 employers couldn't our workers rob?"

"There are foreign terrorists across that line
 who wish to bring our nation down,"
"Yes, and our soldiers are over there killing
 all the jihadists that can be found."

"We're trying to protect our great nation's culture and our way of life."

"What sort of culture do we have to protect with so much anger and strife?"

"We need a wall from gulf to sea to protect the land of the free."

"Sir we already have the FBI and NSA spying on you and me."

I said. "How much do they pay you to protect this invisible line?"

"Well, I earn a very good living, and I'm worth every dime."

"Well, sir, I'm trained as a public school teacher and can barely afford to eat.

I should've signed up to guard this invisible line where our two countries meet."

"I just set out to walk to the village over there below that hill."

"Then you'll have to go to the back of the line and pay the bill."

"You'll need a passport and a visa to cross over or to stay.

To get those vital documents, there are many fees to pay."

"When you cross you'll have to pay for any personal goods you declare.

When you return across the line you'll pay for any goods you bought there."

On that sunny day I decided not to cross that invisible border line.
I didn't want to enrich these men by giving them what was mine.

I hear experts talking of a new global economy all the time.
Still, nation states jealously guard their invisible border lines.

From the International Space Station no lines are visible on continents below,
yet entire armies guard the lines that the paper political maps all show.

Perhaps my children will live in a world where all these lines have disappeared.
Some people say this would be a good thing, while others say it should be feared.

Maybe that which our God didn't create shouldn't be recognized.
He made a single earth for us all, and we're all equal in His eyes.

Alben J. Chamberlain

California Blowing

Summer's on his way out and he's put on quite a show.
Fall is coming on fast and we can expect quite a blow.

Wind

The humidity is dropping and the desert winds stir up the dust.
My sinus pressure is soon rising so medicate myself I must.

    Wind

Soon, it's pouring down through the pass into the valley below.
The wind pushes the hot air before it when it begins to flow.

        Wind

It pushes over the mountain peaks and moans through all the pines.
It flows down slope past the chaparral and crosses highway lines.

            Wind

It's gusts tear the leaves from my trees and blows them all around.
I never see them turn yellow or fall on their own to the ground.

                Wind

The attacking winds rip the shingles from my roof and fills my yard with debris.
It dries out my sun-baked garden and breaks branches from my shade trees.

Wind

It whips trash, leaves and dust into uncovered swimming pools.
It makes all the children hyperactive in the public schools.

    Wind

It blows giant cargo rigs off the freeway like fallen dinosaurs.
It shakes everybody's windows and batters at their doors.

        Wind

It makes homeowners apprehensive with worry about wild fires.
It raises costs to tax payers with all its dangers and risks so dire.

            Wind

The gutters are filled with palm fronds from the gusty wind.
Its steady roaring pressure makes all the palm trees bend.

                Wind

Outdoor events and college classes are canceled when it howls.
Playground time at recess is curtailed, making teachers scowl.

                    Wind

Some folks actually like the wind and are sad when it blows slower.
Those with allergies may lose their minds before it's finally over.

                          Wind

Alben J. Chamberlain

Christmas In The POW Camp
(Christmas Of 1944)

Christmas in a POW Camp, a continent away from home.
The only consolation is being away from the combat zone.

These Italian soldiers are not in California alone.
Several thousand now call this POW Camp home.

My name is Raymond Luna, a prison guard from San Berdoo.
Gradually, as Christmas nears, I sense the war is nearly through.

Many prisoners are trusted to work, for their keep to pay,
laboring hard in local vineyards and orchards almost every day.

They don't lack for food or clothes, but feel dreadfully alone.
For many, this is their third Christmas away from home.

I am told they are my enemy, but I see them as fellow men.
What sort of Christmas comfort or cheer can I send?

I talk to the Bishop at St. Bernardine's Church in San Berdoo.
He has a few ideas about what we might be able to do.

He says, "A Nativity Set and decorations could help to change
 their mood.
A Christmas Mass with a choir singing would change their
 attitude."

Many orchard owners donate cash to build our Nativity Set.
With a few radio announcements, our goals are quickly met.

With help from volunteers, the decorations come to pass.
A large tent is found so we can hold our Christmas Mass.

Crates of donated citrus are taken by volunteers to the camp.
There are smiles on prisoner's faces, despite the rain and damp.

At sundown on Christmas Eve, the Bishop celebrates the Mass with care.
Joyous Christmas music from the choir fills the California winter air.

In December 1944, at our POW camp, Christmas came to captive men,
just like it had to shepherds long ago in the town of Bethlehem.

CHARLOTTE LeVECQUE

Buffalo Stars

Many cultures include beliefs in Spirit Animals, or Spirit Guides. These seek out humans who can benefit from their wisdom and offer it to them. Each animal guide has specific gifts to share. Some of the powers of horse spirits are energy and power. They represent the keeper of partnerships. This is a story about one of them.

He was named Dream Hunter by the warrior that owned his mother. The warrior, Red Sky, had dreamed his black and white mare produced a totally white foal, without a trace of any other color, except for dark eyes, hooves and skin. When the mare led her colt back to the village and Red Sky saw that he was pure white, he called him Dream Hunter. He felt the horse had hunted to find him in his dream. By naming the baby, he welcomed him into the tribe.

Dream Hunter was born at the end of winter. The tribe were still living in the winter camp. Mostly, the mothers and foals spent the days grazing in a large open prairie during the day. Dream Hunter would look at the wide blue sky and wished he could run among the clouds. At night when the black bowl of the sky was dotted with stars the horses were brought closer to camp to dream among the tribe.

One day the camp became animated, people began packing food, dismantling the teepees, and loading equipment on travois or over horse's backs. It was time to move to the summer camp. Dream Hunter's mother was Red Sky's bison hunting horse and he would ride her on the trek, while Dream Hunter would run free at her side,

Once at the summer camp, people began talking about the buffalo that would be coming. When Dream Hunter saw a huge dust cloud, heard grunting, bawling noises, and smelt a pungent, earthy aroma, he knew bison were coming. The buffalo horses became alert and agitated, including Dream Hunter's mother. The colt and other foals were tied up in the camp and the warriors and their buffalo hunting horses went dashing off after the herd.

The foals were nervous as their mother's left. They could see the bison horses cutting into buffalo herd, making fast turns, dodging the horns and yet get close to the beast so their warrior could throw his spear.

Some of the babies struggled and pulled on the ropes holding them and dug in the dirt, being frustrated. Dream Hunter was furious, screaming, pulling more and more until finally he was able to break the rope. He took off racing toward the herd.

He began running behind the herd and calling to his mother. As he ran, he soon caught up and was running alongside the buffalo herd. Some of the buffalo tried to get close to him. They shook their horns as a threat. He dodged and kept running.

By the time he caught up to his mother this hunt was mostly over. There were dead bison all over the plain. The women were already starting to butcher them.

Dream Hunter was breathing hard and his mother was, too. Red Sky was looking at the foal appraisingly. They look into each other's eyes and both knew that Dream Hunter would be a bison hunter, as was his mother.

In the following years Dream Hunter grazed and raced with other foals in winter and summer pastures. They played at chasing each other, running, bucking, and spinning, pretending they were chasing buffalo. When they tired, they took a nap in the warm sun. Dream Hunter grew fleet and strong. Red Sky began riding him and teaching him to run and chase, to charge and dodge among the horse herd and sometimes around the buffalo herds.

Dream Hunter grew as big as his mother, bigger, actually. Then there was a big festival in the camp, with singing, dancing and celebrations. Red Sky's daughter was getting married. Red

Sky put a halter of leather and beads on Dream Hunter's head, eagle feathers in his mane and a buffalo robe over his back. He led the horse to the celebrations and handed the lead rope to the husband of his daughter. This was how Dream Hunter became the bison hunter of the warrior, Grey Owl. They looked at each other knew a new life was open to both of them.

Grey Owl and Dream Hunter were a team now. They learned to trust each other. Dream Hunter learned that Grey Owl would lean in the direction he wanted to travel. Grey Owl learned that his horse really loved racing the wind. At times they almost read each other's mind.

They took part in all bison hunts. They had many buffalo to their credit and were both revered for their skills in hunting. These were good years, Grey Owl's family grew and the tribe was well fed.

Then the blue shirts arrived and were taking the land. They drove off the tribe, away from where the buffalo grazed. The took the summer camp for the farms for their people and felled the trees in the winter camp that had protected the tribe from cold, wind and snow. There had been many skirmishes between the tribe and the blue shirts. They were different than buffalo hunting. The noise from the blue shirts guns was deafening. All men were mounted and many were killed. Many horses died, too, on both sides. In an effort to push back at the blue shirts, many tribes were gathering together. There was to be a large battle in late Spring.

There were many days of fighting around a river and many died. On the fifth day of fighting, Dream Hunter felt Grey Owl fall on his neck and slide down his shoulder. When he spun to look back at him, knew his warrior was dead. He then felt the hard pellets enter his shoulder. He tried to go forward but another pellet hit him. He dropped to his knees, tried to get up, as other shots entered his body. His spirit left his body.

He discovered, he had another destiny, He became a spirit dream hunter. He raced in the night sky, among stars, and moons, and planets. It was like chasing buffalo, fast turns, spirals, and ducking, playing touch and go with celestial bodies.

He lives in the sky, now. Where he seeks the spirit of troubled human souls, who can't sleep because of pain, illness, frustration, anxiety or other sources. He takes them to the stars to offer the calm, comfort and solace of the night sky. They share the partnership of speed and energy hunting buffalo stars.

The humans he seeks always relax in the quiet dark night on his back and behold the world in wonder. When they are at peace he returns them to their beds. They will not remember chasing the buffalo stars, although they may remember a dream where they were flying.

Charlotte LeVecque

Ten

I have ten children. I know that is a lot and sometimes I feel like I don't know what to do. Some of them I gave birth to and some of them are adopted. I can never remember which is which.

We live in a shoebox of a house. It is tiny with four small bedrooms and two baths. The dining room is so small that if the weather is good we eat outdoors on the patio. In bad weather we have to put up an extra table to hold us all. We have a small fenced back yard for the kids to play. A park with swings and slides is not far away.

Most of the bedrooms have two bunk beds in them. I'm trying to give Darius, the oldest at 16, some space, and have a pull out bed in the office. He also has a bunk in the boys' room, along with Brick—called that because of his head of red hair. He is 14. David, age 12, and Billy, age 8, share the room, too.

We have two sets of twin girls, all of them 10. Molly, Penny, Laura, and Bridget. They get along extremely well and share a room with a sign on the door that reads, "If you ain't a twin, you can't git in." The poor English, a sign of their sense of humor. The boys room simply says, "no girls." Suzanne, 8, and Maureen, 7, room with me in a large master bedroom that fits the three beds.

We are a pet loving family. We have a Doberman, Nikko. He is extremely protective of the kids. Mytoy is a tortoise-shell calico cat. Two look-alike hamsters, Frick and Frack, live in the girls' room as twins. Two rabbits, Tweedledum and Tweedledee, who are neutered, live in a hutch outside. A lizard—Godzilla, of course—and three fish, Nemo, Dory, and Moby, in the boys' room round out ten pets for ten kids.

My husband died about three years ago in an auto accident.

He left us pretty well provided for. We are not rich but the kids have always had a roof over their head and food in their belly. Clothes are shared and/or handed down as appropriate. New shoes before school kill me but I try to spread it out over the summer. We have one desktop computer and one iPad. Kids who have homework to do on computer get first choice on computer time. I wish we could get another one, and maybe we can with appropriate planning. Darius has his driver's license now and is very helpful getting the rest of the kids places. I would like to see if we can get him a safe used car. Money is never far from my thoughts, however.

I sent Darius, Molly, Laura and Billy to the grocery store to pick up some cheese for our spaghetti dinner, and salad fixings. When they returned and were unpacking their purchases they handed me a piece of paper and said, "What's this Mom?" I looked at it, in some confusion and then recognized the heading, Power Ball. "It's a lottery ticket", I replied to the kids," and it was drawn yesterday, October 10th." "OOOOHHH," they said their eyes big and bright. "Our lucky number, 10 and look," Molly added, "the power number is 10, too. I bet we won something"

None of us could figure out how the lottery ticket got in the grocery bag, which was one the kids took from home. Eventually we gave up trying to figure out the puzzle.

Can you imagine my surprise, confusion and joy when I took the ticket to the local 7-Eleven and put it through their bar code and stared at the print out? The clerk came over, since I looked like I needed help and with a big smile said, "You won ten thousand dollars".

The kids were thrilled, singing and dancing went on in a big way. They began listing the things they wanted to get. This went on all night, some of us did not sleep that night. I kept trying to think of the best way to spend the money, save for college, look for car, get another computer. I could hear many of the children, whispering through the night.

The next morning as we gathered for breakfast, the kids met

me with, "Mom, we've been talking and since this money was not expected we think we need to give some to special causes". Darius, had become the spokesperson for them, and continued, "We would like to give some to the rabbit rescue where we got the Tweedles. It would help provide for some other orphan bunnies. Also, we would like to give some to foster children, and maybe to one of the programs for homeless people?"

And so they did it again, my kids, when this somewhat old lady who has so many children she doesn't know what to do, ten kids lead the way.

Jessica Lea Morgan

Resurrection Garden

The cactus glistens with ornaments but it is Lenten season.
Metallic graveyard.

Tattered fabric flowers surround crosses and candles.
Grieving ghosts.

Yellow mustard blooms fill the field enfolding the discarded couch.
Spring carpet.

Wind blows torn clothes captured in chain link fences.
Prayer flags.

Vibrant plywood windows on buildings blackened by filth or flame.
Graffiti Guild.

Low grey clouds shroud rain fed mountains.
Resurrection Garden.

JESSICA LEA MORGAN

Scents

The fragrance of mown grass
and you are 12
waking up
in the pink room with slanted walls
ready to go in the pool.

A whiff of a Cabbage Patch doll
and you are five
waking up
on Christmas morning.

I searched for your scent
breathed into your pillow and clothes
after you died
in that room with pink sloping walls
and inhaled nothingness.

Jessica Lea Morgan

electronic dusting

of professional resumes
generates flashbacks
of agonizing choices
perfectly precise pretentious
action verbs.

So
much
minutia.

One page
every
ten years.

Detailed descriptions
weaned
to blips
then a list
then
delete.
Delete.
DELETE.

Maybe editing
removing everything
will stamp out

      memories and regrets
      from decades
          toiling away
                          towards a forgotten goal
which must have been
so important
at the time.

JESSICA LEA MORGAN

Haiku in Wrightwood

Butterfly shadow
dances across flagstone path
spirit visitor

Wind in trees sounds like
the freeways or ocean waves
mist moves through mountains

smell of sap and pine
rustling leaves needles falling
walk pinecone pathway

Jessica Lea Morgan

Quiet

Outside
to
sound bathe
craving respite

train whistles
children screech
parents holler
bicycle gears
rattle
click
cars
backfire like gunshots
horn honking
sirens sound
the undercurrent

of manmade racket
flowing
as one
indistinguishable
noise
a discordant symphony
drowning out
the chirping
buzzing
fluttering

gurgling
rustling
creaking
my soul ached to hear.

The only sounds of nature
coming from a video
on my laptop
which would have been
easier to hear
if I stayed inside.

S. J. Perry

Taking Down the Lights

The Inland Empire sun shines bright,
but the Santa Anas are gusting cold.
It's the day after New Year's,
but the brightly colored lights are as promiseless
as the carols still looping
at any SoCal mall.

As I climb up and down the ladder,
unclipping each section of lights,
I feel it in my quads,
and there's a little hollow behind my sternum.
I'm an old man now,
but I still feel a child's wonder and sadness
as the holidays come and go.

Maybe it's not the holidays themselves
but their reminder that the years
are unreeling.

Taking down the lights
is a forlorn, hopeful act.
As I go
I reel the long string of lights
into the box,
readying them for next year
as I put them away for this.

CINDI PRINGLE

I Don't Wanna

She's got the 'I don't wannas' *bad* today. She can't find a single thing she wants to do. Her mind isn't lighting up with enthusiasm over a-n-y-t-h-i-n-g.

Sitting there in the purple recliner, she's thinking, 'I *should do* something.' But what?

She wonders how she'll feel if, at the end of the day, she doesn't have anything to show for her time. She likes a sense of accomplishment. In fact, she thrives on it.

She picks up the newspaper and glances over the stories. Scanning the headlines or the middle or end of a story, she doesn't read any article completely. Turning the page, she finds the obituaries. She focuses on one smiling face, beaming out from a radiant pink blouse in a photo taken years earlier.

'She's lucky. She's done.'

Maudlin thought, but she finds a fleeting sense of relief in it. No more endless bills to pay, no more dull committee meetings, no more expensive car repairs – the end of the everyday B.S. of life.

As she fantasizes about that sense of release, her mind lazily wanders back to her dream from last night: *I'm swimming off the pier in the ocean. The water feels thick against my arms and legs. The coldness makes my limbs numb and heavy. I don't seem to be making headway as I struggle to push the water behind me. It feels choppy, splashing my face. I peer out over the surface to calculate how much longer before I reach the shore, but I cannot tell. A grain of fear starts to grow within me; I'm tired, but I can't stop. Far away, brightly colored umbrellas on the beach and children frolicking in the sand make it seem like a circus has come to town. I'm alone, far from the merriment.*

'Wait a minute, I've been here before,' she registers, as her mind returns to the present. This is an old, familiar lackluster feeling that years ago would play out in a dismal day of hours lost to motionlessness, brooding, barely eating, and long naps. Friend or foe: She's having a "down" day.

It took many years for her to grasp that an occasional, random admiration for the imagined "carefree" dead was a red flag for the blues.

Who knows what stirred up this hot mess? Ruminations about old regrets, or current resentments percolating just below the surface of consciousness, an emotional cauldron is bubbling up today.

It could be, too, that she's coming down with an illness and doesn't have any symptoms yet. She wonders which comes first, the disease or the dis-ease. Her mind is intuitively attuned to signals from her body; she's learned "the blues" may mean she's sick.

So it's gonna be *tha*t kind of day: Tuesday-*lite*. She'll have to give herself some grace and set aside the feelings of inadequacy when the chores don't get done.

She's gotta honor the 'I don't wannas' one more time.

Cindi Pringle

Mountain Majesty

Earth stretches upward
bluffs crescendo toward peaks
granite thrusts through brush

rugged slopes circle valley
stately crown atop flat land

mountains draw grey clouds
white mist drifts over rocks, plants
lime green moss lines crags

patchy snow dusts timberline
tree roots cling to cliffs' anchor

stones cast carelessly
storm-strewn, tumble down incline
rubble on the road

blue twilight outlines summit
skyline delights in Earth's kiss

Things to do in Hell

Pick flowers
Solve a fiendish Sudoku
Bake double-chocolate chip cookies
Cause a fatal car crash
Stare out the window
Try speed dating

Walk a labyrinth
Call your ex
Scream out from a nightmare
Take a bubble bath
Overcook the turkey
Read your obituary

Start a rumor
Brood
Ask a celebrity for a selfie
Wait for the biopsy results
Negotiate with a debt collector
Lead a group in prayer

Pick up dog poo
Make a wish and throw coins in the fountain
Slaughter a chicken and roast it
Shoplift
Recite "Desiderata" from memory in front of the class
Blame your parents

Remarry your ex
Learn to skydive
Click the link that launches a virus on your computer
Grab a Starbucks to go
Abandon your home in a wildfire
Lie to the priest in confession

Plot to escape from Hell
Give up cable
Take the kids on a hot air balloon ride
Come down with food poisoning
Break the windows with a baseball bat
Savor the last meal before your execution

(Inspired by "Things to Do in Hell" by Chris Martin, 2019)

CAROLYN SNOW

Autumn Nights

Autumn leaves twirl
Twilight brings a crimson sky

Long chilly nights creep early
Pulling me home where
Steamy soup fills our hungry hearts.

Mulled spices perfume the air we
Savor sweet cinnamon apple tart.

Through half open window slats
Orange moon delights
Winking stars that light the night.

Crackling fireplace glows
Warm laughter drifts in the air.
Classical guitar strums softly,
Candles flicker brightly.

Pets sleeping soundly and
Children quilted in soft dreams

Day breaks silently
New dawn slowly peaks her head.
Daylight breaks the spell

Carolyn Snow

Hair with Flair

Hello hair, how do you fair
What is your pleasure today
Long dark curly locks
Or a slick backed, long, smooth, shiny, ponytail
Or perhaps a scarf to reveal your softer side
Twisted and shaped Kente cloth, artfully crowning your mane
Your rich ancestry on full display
The covering removed to reveal thick, curly, beautiful, black hair

Carolyn Snow

The Invited Guest

Thanksgiving is a happy, festive, family time where people gather and celebrate the season. Family and friends come over and bring food, merriment and fun, usually. Flashback to the winter of 2005. I was hosting Thanksgiving dinner, again, and I had recently run into my brother whom none of us had seen in years.

* * * *

"Hello"

"Hi Linda it's me, Alex. I just wanted to call and say hello and see how you are doing."

"Oh! Hi Alex how are you doing I'm surprised to hear from you after all of these years. How are you? How did you get my phone number?"

"I've had your number for years."

"And you're just now calling me after ten years of nobody knowing where you were or how you're doing?"

"Yea, sorry about that. I've been in the military working with the Special Forces. I wasn't allowed to tell anyone where I was or what job I was doing."

Yea right, I thought, brother you probably just got out of the pen.

"Alex, we haven't heard from you in years, ever since you and dad got into that big argument and you left, no one has seen or heard from you in a very long time."

Alex had a way of pushing dad's buttons and arguing with him on a regular basis. Of course the stuff they argued about was usually trivial and unimportant most of the time because they pretty much disagreed about everything just for the sake of being disagreeable. The disagreement usually ended when dad would stand up, grab his keys, and say, "Oh wow Look at the time! I was supposed to be out of here thirty minutes ago."

Or sometimes, to end the conflict, he would abruptly change the conversation to something else like sports or one of his other favorite subjects, his new boat.

Anyway, what ever the reason was I don't remember. I have too many things going on in my own life to try to remember what he was upset about every time he shut down and stopped speaking to everyone. I always tried to cut him some slack since he was younger than me and my three older sisters. I always had a sense that we needed to watch out for him and take care of him because he was the baby of the family.

This Thanksgiving Day, because I hadn't seen him in a while, during our phone conversation I invited him to come over for dinner. He was very excited and said he'd be there. I quickly gave him my address and told him he didn't have to bring anything. He said he'd bring something, but he wasn't sure what.

Thanksgiving Day arrived and as mom, dad, my sisters, brother in law, cousins and the rest of the family began to arrive I was busy getting everything ready and preparing to put the food on the table. Mom and Debbie, my sister, helped out. While we were getting everything ready and setting the table I suddenly heard my dad say.

"Oh my goodness, what are you doing here? Hey honey!" He said to my mom excitedly, "Alex is here."

At the sound of that announcement other relatives started going to the front room to greet him and say hello as he walked into the front hallway. It was such a surprise for everyone that I was happy I had invited him. It really felt good to see him and to see everyone's response.

However, that happy, festive feeling didn't last very long. It turns out that Alex didn't actually call me out the blue, on a whim. As the men folk began to settle in and watch the football game I could overhear my brother saying to my dad.

"I can pay you back in a few months, I just need to borrow

two thousand dollars so I can move and put a deposit down on a new apartment."

What in the world was he doing? Two thousand dollars! Alex was asking dad if he could borrow two-thousand dollars! I thought as I was trying to tend to my guests and listen to his conversation with my dad. By then the white Zinfandel was flowing, most everyone was watching the football game, others had started a card game at the table in the den, the kids were outside running around in the backyard and the thanksgiving party was in full swing.

Oh Lord, please don't let an argument start. I prayed silently to myself as the nervousness and anxiety began to creep up on me, this was not going well. Maybe I should have invited him to a quiet Sunday dinner instead of something as big and festive as Thanksgiving dinner where everybody showed up

"Would anyone like some dessert?" I announced. "The choices are sweet potato pie, chocolate cake, vanilla ice cream, fresh fruit..."

The heated discussion began to calm down a little with the dessert announcement.

"Linda, I'll serve the dessert."

Thank goodness I thought as my knees began to grow weak at the thought of a family fight after all of these years of peace, big sister Diane to the rescue. Diane was the one who always came through. She could sense trouble and come to the rescue at a moment's notice.

"Alex," I called to my brother. "Here's some sweet potato pie and hot tea for you."

He didn't hear me. He was upset now because dad turned him down and said he couldn't lend him the money. What a set up, I can't believe my brother came over here to the Thanksgiving party not with the intent of celebrating the season and spending happy times with his family, but he came with the intent of asking dad for money. It was obvious to everyone, especially my dad, that Alex had come here for this reason. He had not called me out of the blue, asking dad for money was the reason he came over for Thanksgiving dinner that day.

"Son if you just came from the military after being gone for over ten years you should have some money, housing, benefits and everything else that goes along with military service." Said dad.

I realized that I invited him by mistake thinking that it would be a good thing since none of us had seen him in such a long time. It started off okay, how could I have known that after all the years that had passed by he was still the same person he was when he left. I tried not to be upset with him, but I had to fight the guilty feelings I had about the way things turned out. I gave myself credit for trying. Trying to bring him back into the fold, to the family so that we could all begin to welcome Alex back into the family and spend time together again like we used to. But I guess it was just not meant to be.

BETH WINOKUR

A Response to Dr. Angelou's Pulse

This morning
Permits only substance
Find, no sugary pastries at this table
An efficient spread,
Good for the heart; bran and oats
You're welcome.

Yesterday's dinner; shameful and sickly
Denial
Ensures tonight's meal, abundant
with expired fruit

The bold pulse.
Names both natures;
Peace and War
The Rock, the River, the Tree
Advise which to nurture
And which to starve

Familiar message
Spoken once by each quiet heart
Without stutter.
In song, in picture, in story, in philosophy, in science,
In animal friend's ears from each child's mouth
Yet lost and forgotten,
By constant chatter
Ego, envy, greed, power.

Recognition of our best nature
The one silently agreed upon
Yet,
Held a rung below
the savior profit
Yet still,
Light candles, in a shameful
Silent protest

The morning's light exposes
This casual existence
Only earth to stand on, here
No grand podium
Not for any breath,
Not ever
hosted by the Rock, the River, the Tree
No exception
No refuge
In self-proclaimed specialness
Peace lives, in that truth

The Gift
Sings the new day
One song after another
Titled Acceptance,
Titled Freedom,
Titled Choice.

The poet prays
Choose humanity's best
Assemble a choir,
Harmonize
The Rock, the River, the Tree

BETH WINOKUR

Across the Water –No Boat Required

Hydrilla and Cattail slide and tangle on
Driven legs
Creatively fueled by
Leeches, snakes, rejected alligators
angry they are in the wrong water

The island beams
Dreamy, wild, romance,
A confined freedom

Judgmental peers, sure
But the right kind
"Be cool," they say

Sun follows his strict schedule
While Moon
Escapes her duties
Leaving the night to a few lit dots
Far
From here

Boys come by boat
Gas cans and beer
Girls laugh,
different
Rhythm, pitch, timber

Murky water invites

Copperheads, electric eels and
That same discarded pet alligator

Friends reassure
A ride in some handsome boat
Pleasant, comfortable, secure
Across the lake
"Trust," they chant

The boys, their bookcase
Equal in capacity
height, width, depth
Yet, these shelves are
Void of any familiar text

Conversations
Stir settled dust,
But cannot fill the space
It is said that comes later
Maybe
Doubtful

Judgmental
"Not cool," they cry
They've come for praise and
Love
But were presented with
Eye rolls and silence
"Can't work with, that," says bitter lips

Free from their howls
and wasted breath

Free from approval
and invitation, to
board their lame drifting skiff

Free, to dive
into murk
Vivacious,
And swim—
at peace with
Hydrilla, Cattails and that odd alligator

Author Biographies

Margit Anderrson was born in Sweden and has lived in Hemet for the last 15 years. She was always interested in literature and writing. Since she retired, she attended UC Riverside and obtained a degree in Anthropology. She now volunteers at the Western Center of Natural History in Hemet. Margit enjoys reading, traveling and learning new things.

At 90 years old, **Sam Barclay** served in the US Army during the Korean war. After working for Chicken of The Sea, he obtained a Business Administration degree, later owning pet stores in southern California and in Georgia.

V. K. Begley attends the 'Fiction & Non-Fiction' writing workshop at The Janet Goeske Center in Riverside, CA. She is a regular member of 'Underground Writers Unite'; a novel writing group; where she 'presents' subjects of interest to novelists. She has completed a science-fiction trilogy and NANOWRIMO 2019.

Originally from East Los Angeles, **Mary Rodriguez Briggs** has lived in Riverside for 30 years celebrating her emerging voice as a first generation Mexican-American and a Hispanic woman living in an Anglo world and a female of her generation.

Beyond fluid movements of Tai Chi Chih, former coastal California artist, **Georgette Buckley**, B.A. Studio Art, fondly recalls teaching painting, attending archaeology lectures amongst Roman ruins and backpacking misty, green Ireland. Selected for the 2007 Myriad Journal, she and her husband of 38 years thrive in Inlandia.

A metastatic breast cancer survivor, a proactive community leader in the Inland Empire and multiple published author, **Celena-Diana (OceanMoonSpirit) Bumpus** has been teaching creative writing classes since 2010. Visit her profile for her social media links under @oceanmoonspirit:
https://m.facebook.com/celenadiana/
https://m.facebook.com/islands4writers/

Alben Chamberlain was born in San Bernardino, California on May 22, 1953. He has lived in the Inland Empire for most of his life. He attended San Bernardino Valley College, and received a BA degree from BYU-Hawaii. He earned an MBA from The American Graduate School in Glendale, Arizona as well as several teaching credentials from The University of California-Riverside.

Natalie Michele Champion received her BS Degree in Business Administration from UCR and a teaching credential from San Francisco State. After participating in poetry workshops in Riverside, Natalie submitted her poems to Inlandia. She lives in San Francisco with her husband, Rick, and two cats, Princess Tabitha and Milo Morris.

Rick Champion says, "I gather feelings that I weave into mosaics. I have been accused of exaggeration. I plead guilty. I know what came down with Lady Godiva, passed to me through her own lips. Curious? Wait and hear."

Jessica Carrillo's Inlandia Writing Workshops and Celena's writing classes have given **Sylvia Nelson Clarke** an appreciation of her fellow writers and opportunity to build friendships. The encouragement received has strengthened her desire to share her blessings through writing poetry and stories—hers and those of others.

Wil Clarke wishes to thank Jessica Carrillo, his Inlandia Workshop leader, and Celena Bumpus, his fiction/non-fiction writing teacher, for their continuous, strong encouragement to write. Long may they live! He won a NaNoWriMo novel writing challenge in November 2019.

Deborah Clifton lives in Riverside, Ca. She is a student of the Inlandia Goeske Poets In Motion class. She is publishing her first poetry collection through Islands For Writers.

Deenaz P. Coachbuilder, Ph.D. is a writer whose poems, commentaries and essays have been published internationally. Her two books of poems, *Metal Horse And Shadows: A Soul's Journey* and

Imperfect Fragments, have been received with critical acclaim in the U.S. and abroad. Deenaz is an educator, artist, writer and environmental advocate.

Carlos Cortés is professor emeritus of history at the University of California, Riverside. His recent books include his memoir, *Rose Hill: An Intermarriage before Its Time*, and a book of poetry, *Fourth Quarter: Reflections of a Cranky Old Man*, which received honorable mention in the 2017 International Latino Book Awards.

Laurel Vermilyea Cortés faithfully attends Inlandia Institute workshops, and is an occasional contributor to the Inlandia column in the Riverside Press-Enterprise. She favors essays in her writing, and likes to include historical and literary dimensions. Laurel often aims her studies and remembrances at her family, especially her four millennial grandchildren.

Aaron Craig lives in Riverside, Ca. He attends the Inlandia Goeske Poets In Motion class.

A coastal native of the west, **Diana Dolphin** lives in Riverside, Ca, where she haunts all-u-can-eat sushi bars for the taste of brine she misses living in the desert. On rare sightings you may find her dancing in the rain or lounging poolside.

Jerry Ellingson lives in Redlands, California. Meeting with the family of Joslyn Joy Writers in Redlands is one of the most fulfilling activities of her week. Here, Jerry's goal is to record family stories so her family will not only have photos and statistics, but stories that should be told so future generations can understand the thoughts and feelings of those that preceded them as they lived through history. She is a retired teacher with a Bachelor's degree in Dance and English. Her Master's degree is in education. The greatest joys in her life have been teaching Graphic Design and Computer to adults and her role as a mother and grandmother.

In 1952, **Chuck Farrar** was born in Pasadena and has resided in Southern California his entire life. Upon graduating from UCRiverside, Chuck worked as a crop entomologist for forty years. Retired, he enjoys sailing, the rewards, power, and freedom of volunteerism, and writing with and for friends and family.

Nan Friedley is a retired special education teacher and graduate of Ball State University, Muncie, IN. Her writing has been published in a poetry chapbook, *Short Bus Ride* by Bad Knee Press, *Indiana Voice Journal*, *Writing from Inlandia* anthologies, and *Three* a nonfiction anthology collection by PushPen Press. Nan participates in the Riverside Inlandia workshop.

Hazel Fuller is a native Californian. She resides in Redlands where she attended school. During her junior and senior years she worked in the school library. This experience prepared her for a job at the San Bernardino County Library where she worked for two years. After moving to Ventura she worked in the Ventura County Library while attending night classes at Ventura City College. She worked many years in libraries for the Dept. of Defense and Dept. of Interior. Hazel joined the Joslyn Joy Writers in January 2018. Besides writing she enjoys reading about and restoring Victorian houses.

Christina Guillén is the author of the historical fiction novel, *Cenquizqui*, in which a biracial conquistador relinquishes his riches to discover his indigenous roots. Christina practices under the Lakota tradition, Oklevueha Native American Church, and Tateya Topa altar. Mitakuye Oyasin. Ometeotl.

Renee Gurley, MA, MFA, is a writer and English teacher. Her works have appeared in *Coping Magazine, Midwifery Today, Gemini Magazine* and *HitchLitReview* She hosts RgurleyRevolution, a podcast sharing stories of women around the world. Her other writings can be found at *The Desert Diaries*. She attends the Corona Workshop with Andrea Ferguson.

Tim Hatch writes poetry that explores themes of abuse, fragility, and our human obligation to one another. He earned his MFA at Cal State San Bernardino, and his poetry has appeared in *East Jasmine Review, The Vehicle, Touch: The Journal of Healing, Apeiron Review*, and *Cholla Needles*. He teaches composition at Riverside

City College, and Cal State San Bernardino. His collection of poetry, which has gone through several titles, will be forthcoming whenever he gets his act together.

Richard Hess is a retired OBGYN physician. He practiced in Alaska for 41 years and is now living in Redlands. He presented this writing at the Joslyn Senior Center Creative Writing course with Mae Marinello.

MaryAnn Holmes lives in Riverside, Ca. She is a student in the Inlandia Goeske Poets In Motion class.

Rosalie Hruska is a member of the Joslyn Joyful Writers at the Senior Center in Redlands. She is an octogenarian who has experienced the loves and losses that a long life can bring. Writing about those experiences bring comfort and closure.

Connie Jameson, a 50 year resident of Riverside, California, loves the climate and beauty of nature in our Inland Empire. Ms. Jameson enjoys reading, travel, antiques, theater and Toastmasters. She is published in the "*Heart of _____*" series (*Heart of a Mother, Heart of the Holidays, Heart of a Toastmaster*).

Born in Barbados, **Joan M. Jones** is a Vietnam era, USAF veteran. In 1987, she graduated with a Doctorate of Pharmacy, retiring from the Department of Public Health in 2014. Now she pursues her passion of writing poetry and stories.

Charlotte LeVecque has been attending Inlandia Workshop under the direction of Romaine Washington since 2017.

Robin Longfield was born in Chamblee, Georgia, but grew up in Midway City, CA, a very small unincorporated area between Huntington Beach, and Westminster. She is a graduate of Fountain Valley High School, and received a B.A. in English/Creative Writing from U.C. Irvine. In September, 2019, Robin retired after 30+ years in the real estate financing field. She is grateful for her long-suffering husband, John, her 2 amazing, beautiful daughters, and all of her family and friends. She believes in adventures, magic, laughter, and the power of words to change, inspire, and enlighten.

Florence Lucero lives in Riverside, Ca. She is a student of the Inlandia Goeske Poets In Motion class.

Phyllis Maynard has been retired for several years, the loving widow of Douglas and mom to Pam, Danny, Mark and Toby. Writing every chance she gets! In 1988, her poem appeared in the *American Poetry Anthology*. She is currently working on an illustrated children's book about four Dalmatians.

Lawyer by trade and poet at heart, **Jessica Lea Morgan** is a New York transplant thriving in the Inland Empire. She believes that poetry should be relatable and accessible. Jessica participates in The 52 Project at Riverside Art Museum and local workshops through Inlandia, Emerging Urban Poets, *Rattle*, and Stillpoint.

Marlene Mossestad lives in Riverside, Ca. Mrs. Mossestad's biographical essay on Eliza Tibbets, "Cover and McCoy and the Navel Orange" was published in the Riverside Historical Society Journal. She is a student of the Inlandia Goeske Poets In Motion class.

Cindi Neisinger believes curiosity will lead you to your passions. She did not start off with the intention of writing. However, after many writing classes, throughout the Inland Empire, she was hooked. Currently, she is writing short stories and a screenplay. She also, serves on the Inlandia Institute Advisory Council.

Gary Neuharth lives in Redlands, California where he is a member of the Joslyn Writers Group. He has studied art, sculpture and writing at San Bernardino College, La Sierra College and Loma Linda University. Gary was in the Air Force in the late 1950s. While in the Air Force he worked as a technical illustrator in Loan, France. He also taught art in service clubs and exhibited his paintings in Paris and Venice Beach, California. The Bohemian life and the Beat Generation have inspired Gary's art and writing. Gary has published more than a hundred poems, many of which have been included in his art exhibits.

Geri Olayan lives in Riverside, Ca. She is a student in the Inlandia Goeske Poets In Motion class. She is currently publishing her first book.

S. J. Perry grew up in Kansas, where he studied at Emporia State University and the University of Kansas. A retired high school English teacher, he has lived in the San Gorgonio Pass since 1985.

Cindi Pringle is returning to youthful interests in creative writing and illustrating after a career in broadcast journalism and university administration. She is a long-time volunteer at the Mary S. Roberts Pet Adoption Center, where her work includes making pet therapy visits to patients at an acute-care facility.

Phyllis Ahpuk Reis was born in Gadsden Alabama—a baby Boomer. In 1957, Reis' family moved to Riverside, California She is the oldest of three siblings. In March 1975, she was hired by Riverside Countty's Sheriff's Department where she worked jail patrol and the courts. She retired in 2016.

Kristine Ann Shell lives in Redlands, California, where she participates in the Joslyn Writers Group. Kristine is a retired school administrator and teacher. She holds a Bachelor's degree in English and Secondary Education. She also holds Masters degrees in Elementary Reading and School Administration. Kristine joined the Inlandia Institute in October, 2016.

Donna Slezak lives in Riverside, Ca. She is a student in the Inlandia Goeske Poets In Motion class.

Carolyn Snow is an educator, artist, and writer. In her spare time she enjoys writing short stories and poetry. She received her Master of Arts in Educational Administration from the University of Redlands in 2003. She also enjoys camping, outdoor activities and spending time with her grandchildren.

Heather Takenaga is a daydreamer and hungry reader who is re-igniting her childhood love for writing. A graduate of the now defunct Arts Institute of San Diego and online volunteer for many nonprofits. She is a student in CelenaDiana's creative writing class at the Janet Goeske Foundation & Senior Center.

Vicki Urrunaga lives in Riverside, Ca.

Gudelia Vaden (Delia), a retired preschool teacher, has a BA degree in Liberal Studies with Bilingual-Bicultural Emphasis from CSU San Bernardino. She lives in Riverside with husband, Tom, and has two grown children, Natalie and Patrick. Delia loves writing and has been published in the Inlandia Anthology since 2015.

Thomas Vaden (Tom) is a statistician with a MS degree in Mathematics from the University of Missouri Columbia. Tom talks about his St. Louis roots as he introduces Grandpa Bert in this anthology. Tom lives in Riverside with his wife Delia.

Alan VanTassel is an aspiring writer who lives in Redlands, CA with his wife, Sarah, and three Labradors. Alan has contributed to Inlandia twice in the past. Alan is a retired 38-year teacher who taught in the Colton and Banning school districts.

Sarah VanTassel has a BA from UCR; MA and a Teaching credential from CSUSB. Her career included working as a Disability Management Coordinator at LLUMC and UCR and teaching Special Education. Publications include *Los Angeles Time*s and the *American Wanderer.* Sarah lives in Redlands, Ca.

Frances J. Vásquez is native to the Inland region and educated in local schools, RCC, and UC Riverside. An aficionada of arts and letters, she loves attending and organizing cultural events. She serves on the Inlandia institute board of directors and the Multicultural Council of the Riverside Museum Associates.

Born in Chihuahua, Mexico, **Jose Luis Vizcarra** is a Vietnam War, US Army veteran. After using his GI Bill to pay for thirteen years of college education, he taught elementary school and adult ESL for 33 years. He is currently writing two books on financial education.

Jack Wilde grew up along the coast of Southern California and currently lives in Riverside. An avid American West Coast historian, he has traveled across Mexico, working in the Yucatan and driving the backroads of the Baja Peninsula as well as the and

American Southwest deserts for decades, taking any dirt road less traveled whenever possible. He is a student of the Inlandia Goeske Poets In Motion class.

Bobbie Walters lives in Riverside, Ca. She is a student of the Inlandia Goeske Poets In Motion class.

A native of Southern California specifically the Inland Empire region, **Beth Winokur** writes fiction and poetry. Her published works include: *Three Stories: Itch*, (2019) "Second Sun" (A short story in *Bubble off Plumb: An Anthology* 2018), *The Adventures of Abby and Sofia* (2014) and *Sunshine in Darkness* (2013).

About Inlandia Institute

Inlandia Institute is a regional literary non-profit and publishing house. We seek to bring focus to the richness of the literary enterprise that has existed in this region for ages. The mission of the Inlandia Institute is to recognize, support, and expand literary activity in all of its forms in Inland Southern California by publishing books and sponsoring programs that deepen people's awareness, understanding, and appreciation of this unique, complex and creatively vibrant region.

The Institute publishes books, presents free public literary and cultural programming, provides in-school and after school enrichment programs for children and youth, holds free creative writing workshops for teens and adults, and boot camp intensives. In addition, every two years, the Inlandia Institute appoints a distinguished jury panel from outside of the region to name an Inlandia Literary Laureate who serves as an ambassador for the Inlandia Institute, promoting literature, creative literacy, and community. Laureates to date include Susan Straight (2010-2012), Gayle Brandeis (2012-2014), Juan Delgado (2014-2016), Nikia Chaney (2016-2018), and Rachelle Cruz (2018-2020).

To learn more about the Inlandia Institute, please visit our website at www.InlandiaInstitute.org.

Other Inlandia Books

Care: Stories by Christopher Records

San Bernardino, Singing, by Nikia Chaney

Facing Fire: Art, Wildfire, and the End of Nature in the New West by Douglas McCulloh

Writing from Inlandia: Work from the Inlandia Creative Writing Workshops, an annual anthology

In the Sunshine of Neglect: Defining Photographs and Radical Experiments in Inland Southern California, 1950 to the Present by Douglas McCulloh

Henry L. A. Jekel: Architect of Eastern Skyscrapers and the California Style by Dr. Vincent Moses and Catherine Whitmore

Orangelandia: The Literature of Inland Citrus by Gayle Brandeis

While We're Here We Should Sing by The Why Nots

Go to the Living by Micah Chatterton

No Easy Way: Integrating Riverside Schools - A Victory for Community by Arthur L. Littleworth

Hillary Gravendyk Prize poetry series

The Silk the Moths Ignore by Bronwen Tate
    Winner of the 2019 National Hillary Gravendyk Prize

Remyth: A Postmodernist Ritual by Adam Martinez
    Winner of the 2019 Regional Hillary Gravendyk Prize

Former Possessions of the Spanish Empire by Michelle Peñaloza
    Winner of the 2018 National Hillary Gravendyk Prize

All the Emergency-Type Structures by Elizabeth Cantwell
    Winner of the 2018 Regional Hillary Gravendyk Prize

Our Bruises Kept Singing Purple by Malcolm Friend
    Winner of the 2017 National Hillary Gravendyk Prize

Traces of a Fifth Column by Marco Maisto
    Winner of the 2016 National Hillary Gravendyk Prize

God's Will for Monsters by Rachelle Cruz
    Winner of the 2016 Regional Hillary Gravendyk Prize
    Winner of the 2018 American Book Award

Map of an Onion by Kenji C. Liu
    Winner of the 2015 National Hillary Gravendyk Prize

All Things Lose Thousands of Times by Angela Peñaredondo
    Winner of the 2015 Regional Hillary Gravendyk Prize

www.ingramcontent.com/pod-product-compliance
Lightning Source LLC
Chambersburg PA
CBHW051038160426
43193CB00010B/981